continuing professional develc
in education

CPD: Learning to Think, Thinking to Learn

An introduction to thinking skills from
Nursery to Secondary

Dr Margaret Kirkwood

Series editor: Brian Boyd

Published in association with the
Times Educational Supplement Scotland

Hodder Gibson

A MEMBER OF THE HODDER HEADLINE GROUP

The Publishers would like to thank the following for permission to reproduce copyright material:

Acknowledgements
Artworks by Tony Wilkins Design

Every effort has been made to trace all copyright holders, but if any have been inadvertently overlooked the Publishers will be pleased to make the necessary arrangements at the first opportunity.

Although every effort has been made to ensure that website addresses are correct at time of going to press, Hodder Gibson cannot be held responsible for the content of any website mentioned in this book. It is sometimes possible to find a relocated web page by typing in the address of the home page for a website in the URL window of your browser.

Orders: please contact Bookpoint Ltd, 130 Milton Park, Abingdon, Oxon OX14 4SB. Telephone: (44) 01235 827720. Fax: (44) 01235 400454. Lines are open 9.00–6.00, Monday to Saturday, with a 24-hour message answering service. Visit our website at www.hoddereducation.co.uk. Hodder Gibson can be contacted direct on: Tel: 0141 848 1609; Fax: 0141 889 6315; email: hoddergibson@hodder.co.uk

© Margaret Kirkwood 2005
First published in 2005 by
Hodder Gibson, a member of the Hodder Headline Group
2a Christie Street
Paisley PA1 1NB

Impression number   10 9 8 7 6 5 4 3 2 1
Year   2010 2009 2008 2007 2006 2005

Cover illustration by David Parkin.
Typeset by Transet Limited, Coventry, England.
Printed and bound in Great Britain by CPI Bath.

A catalogue record for this title is available from the British Library

ISBN-10: 0-340-88994-2
ISBN-13: 978-0-340-889-947

About the Author

Dr Margaret Kirkwood is Reader in Education at the University of Strathclyde. She began her career as a mathematics teacher and then became involved in teacher education and national curriculum development. She has extensive experience of teaching, curriculum development and research on the enhancement of pupils' thinking, understanding, problem solving and learning strategies through using an infusion approach. She is a past-president of the Scottish Educational Research Association and Secretary General of the European Educational Research Association.

Acknowledgements

I am grateful to Professor Brian Boyd as editor for his great patience, good humour and sound guidance. Above all, I would like to commend my two sons, Andrew and David, for their consideration towards me during the writing of this book. It is dedicated to Andrew and David.

Foreword

The *Times Educational Supplement Scotland* is delighted to be associated with the publication of this prestigious new series of books devoted to key areas in the field of continuing professional development.

Since the newspaper's birth in 1965, we have always attempted to inform, educate, and occasionally entertain the Scottish teaching profession, as well as to encourage dialogue between all educational sectors. In recent years, our commitment to the concept of encouraging educationists to constantly reflect – and act – upon best practice has been most tangibly evident in the provision of an annual CPD supplement. This offers full and detailed examination of developments in CPD from both Scottish and international contexts, and we attempt to share best practice in a manner that is both accessible and valuable.

This series of books is another testimony of our commitment to CPD. Drawing on the experience of foremost Scottish practitioners, each book attempts to offer academic rigour with a lightness of delivery that is too often found wanting in the weightier tomes that populate many educational libraries, and which are consequently left unread, except by those approaching examinations – or job interviews.

In short, we hope that these books will be welcomed in the groves of academe; but we also believe that they deserve to be read – and acted upon – by a much wider audience: those teachers across Scotland, nursery, primary and secondary, who deliver the curriculum on a daily basis to our young people.

Neil Munro
Editor, *Times Educational Supplement Scotland*

Contents

Preface

The key message of this book is that schools do not need to invest in expensive resource packs in order to be successful at developing pupils' thinking. Teachers' own ideas may be more appropriate, and more appealing, to their pupils! There is scope to be creative when planning lessons, and teachers can avoid being 'boxed-in' to a particular resource.

A modest start can be made in any school where teachers have familiarised themselves with the key principles and strategies which underpin successful thinking skills interventions. Teaching thinking involves *guiding and supporting pupils to improve the quality of their thinking*. In order to achieve this, these principles and strategies need to be applied in ways which are suited to your pupils and matched to their curriculum.

There are suggestions for activities (labelled *Thinking points*) incorporated into every chapter and a list of suggested further reading at the end of each. Where there are references to 'lessons' or 'topics', this is not intended to imply a particular way of organising your teaching. Whatever your teaching circumstances, these suggestions should be of value to you and the pupils and colleagues with whom you work. You may not have day-to-day responsibility for teaching a whole class or classes if your role is to provide support for learning or if you are a school manager, in which case there are other ways in which you may be able to put ideas into practice, perhaps through working with individual pupils or groups, co-operative teaching, or in a staff development role. You may be a student teacher, in which case, during your school placement, you could discuss with the class teacher and your tutor how to incorporate some of the ideas into your lessons.

As you reach the end of each chapter and before moving on to the next, you may find it helpful to consider your response to each of the following questions:

1 Did all of the chapter make sense to you?
2 Did you encounter any new ideas?
3 Which are the most interesting and relevant ideas?
4 Which reservations do you have about the ideas contained in the chapter?
5 Which further questions do you have about teaching thinking?

1 An introduction to teaching thinking

> In a classroom culture of thinking, the spirit of good thinking is everywhere. There is the sense that "everyone is doing it", that everyone – including the teacher – is making the effort to be thoughtful, inquiring and imaginative …
> **Shari Tishman, David Perkins and Eileen Jay 1995: p.2**

This chapter begins by addressing the question of why schools should focus strongly on developing pupils' thinking. This is discussed with reference to educational policies and the school curriculum in Scotland for pupils aged from three upwards. Pupils do all different types of thinking, and engage in all different types of thinking tasks, both in and out of school. Of course, some exercises are too routine and do not demand much thinking from pupils, and so they would not count as real 'thinking tasks'. These routine exercises may be there for a different purpose, for example, to give practice at a new skill or procedure. Schools and teachers need to be as clear as possible about the types of thinking to be focused on explicitly during lessons. It is useful to consider how much opportunity there is for pupils to develop a range of thinking skills through the way the present curriculum is taught. Two important aspects of developing pupils' thinking are encouraging a language of thinking in the classroom, and making thinking more 'visible' and open to scrutiny.

Why teach thinking?

Learning to think well is crucially important for your pupils' academic achievements and their lives beyond school, both now and in the future. Teachers have a vital role to play in guiding and supporting all of their pupils to become better thinkers.

An education forum held in 2000 and organised by the Scottish Executive Education Department (SEED) had as its theme *Teaching Thinking Skills*. The forum addressed questions such as, 'What are thinking skills?', 'How can they be useful?', and, 'Can they be taught?' These are among the questions which this book is designed to help you examine in relation to your own teaching situation. To accompany the forum, a review of recent research on teaching thinking was commissioned from the Scottish Council for Research in Education (SCRE). It's author was Valerie Wilson (see Wilson 2000a). Recent research evidence from many relevant sources and the practical experiences of teachers will be drawn upon to identify the key principles to guide your classroom practice and important issues to consider at the classroom, whole school and national level.

Teaching thinking is regarded as important by educators throughout the world. Robert Swartz and Sandra Parks are two educational researchers from the US who have worked closely with teachers to develop an approach to *infusing* the teaching of critical and creative thinking into the content of the school curriculum. They say:

> good thinking is essential in meeting the challenge of living in a technologically oriented, multicultural world. ... knowledgeable thinkers have a better chance of taking charge of their lives and achieving personal advancement and fulfilment. Our students must be prepared to exercise critical judgment and creative thinking to gather, evaluate, and use information for effective problem solving and decision-making in their jobs, in their professions and in their lives.
>
> (Swartz and Parks 1994: p.3)

There is a clear focus here on preparing pupils adequately for the lives they will lead beyond school. Notice that the term, 'knowledgeable thinkers', is used. Frequently the question of which is more important for present-day education – content or process – is debated; by content is meant the substance of the curriculum, and by process is meant the skills and strategies that pupils bring to bear when learning the curriculum, such as communication skills, learning strategies, problem-solving and thinking skills. It is clear that Swartz and Parks place value on both – content and process are not in competition with each other; instead they go hand in hand. It is a question of getting the balance right. I like to put it another way: thinking is always thinking about something, and the prime candidate for pupils to think about in school is the curriculum. This dual emphasis on content and process leads naturally towards an *infusion approach* to teaching thinking, in which thinking skills are blended into lessons and topics.

Of course, it is very important that the curriculum itself is made relevant to young people's lives, otherwise, as every teacher knows, it is an uphill struggle to get pupils interested in learning it. How to bring topics alive and get pupils actively engaged in their learning are two of the biggest challenges that teachers face day to day. It is also very important for teachers to hold a positive view on the prospects for *all* of their pupils to develop better thinking skills, irrespective of any 'ability labels' that may be attached to individual pupils or classes.

There are references to thinking skills in recent policy statements. The National Priorities in Education, embodied in the *Standards in Scotland's Schools Act 2000*, include Learning for Life, which is defined in the following terms: 'to equip pupils with the foundation skills, attitudes and expectations necessary to prosper in a changing society and to encourage creativity and ambition.' Although the foundation skills are not specified in this brief statement, one can surmise that thinking skills must figure prominently. A changing society implies the need for flexible thinkers who are responsive to change. Encouraging creativity implies the need to build the learners' capacity to be inventive and to look at situations from new angles. Encouraging ambition implies the need for learners to set high personal goals and to remain focused on these goals.

Other references to thinking skills can be found in national curriculum advice. *A Curriculum Framework for Children 3–5* www.ltscotland.org.uk/earlyyears/framechildren3to5.asp has this to say about young children as learners:

> Young children come to early years settings as active, experienced learners with a natural curiosity. They are unique individuals eager to make sense of their world, to develop relationships and to extend their skills. Children develop understanding in many different ways but they learn best in an environment where they feel safe, secure, confident and have opportunities for enjoyment. Children deepen awareness of themselves as learners by planning, questioning and reflecting. They consolidate this learning when they have the time and space to engage in activities in depth. They develop theories through investigation, first-hand experience, talk and play.

Play makes a powerful contribution to children's learning. It provides opportunities for children to:

- make sense of real-life situations
- develop awareness of themselves and others
- explore, investigate and experiment
- be actively involved in learning
- draw and test their conclusions
- develop self-confidence
- express their ideas and feelings in many different ways
- inhabit imagined situations
- act out and come to terms with experiences at home or with friends
- be solitary, quiet and reflective
- collaborate with others
- take the initiative on their own terms
- develop relationships
- practise skills
- consolidate previous learning
- be challenged in new learning.

Many 'thinking words' appear within this short description, such as reflecting and imagining. Also many activities are listed here which involve thinking, for example, questioning, making sense of real-life situations, and drawing and testing conclusions. Developing good social skills involves thinking, since it requires considering another person's point of view or feelings and deciding on how to respond appropriately. Thus this short extract serves as a very good example of the important place given to developing children's thinking in the early years of education. Learning to think well is not just for older pupils!

Thinking point 1
Preferably with a colleague, choose a key aspect of the 3–5 curriculum *or* an area of the 5–14 curriculum *or* a Standard Grade or Higher Still course. Identify, from the relevant documentation, the thinking skills which are mainly focused upon.

What do we mean by teaching thinking?

Children already use a variety of types of thinking in their everyday lives. Does it therefore make any sense to talk about teaching thinking if it is something that we all do naturally? Let's take an everyday example. When pals, on the way home from school, decide to have a game of football at the outdoor pitches rather than play a video game, their decision may have been influenced by a number of factors. They may have predicted that the weather will stay dry. They may have decided on football because none of them would be left out whereas only three or four could take part in the video game. They may have had energy to burn off after spending most of the day sitting in class and so they chose the more active pursuit. Perhaps they predicted that they wouldn't be allowed inside to play a video game before doing their homework, whereas they could delay going home, and therefore put off doing homework till later, by playing football! Maybe one kid was dominant in the group and he decided on football and everyone else just went along with the idea. But let's assume that it was a joint decision. When the group *selected from among the two alternatives* they must first have *generated these two possibilities*. They must have *weighed up* which was the better choice, taking the circumstances into account.

Robert Sylwester, one of the foremost interpreters of brain research for educators, marvels at the thinking capabilities of young learners:

> Comparison and classification are monumental cognitive capabilities. They're at the absolute heart of language (our language being nothing more than the verbalization of 500,000 categories). Put 50 maple leaves and one oak leaf on a table and ask 4-year-olds to indicate which one is different. They will typically point to the oak leaf, which is the wrong answer, because all 51 leaves differ from each other. The remarkable thing is that the children are humanly correct, since the oak leaf is more different from the maple leaves than the maple leaves are from each other. It just blows me away to realize that no one really teaches young children to make that kind of discrimination – and it's so essential to everything we do cognitively.
>
> There simply must be a powerful innate system already on line as language emerges. Educators need to be aware of that and respectful of it. We mustn't assume that children will never be able to think if we don't give them workbook exercises in thinking skills.
>
> (Brandt 2001: p.173)

However we know from our personal experience that not all thinking tasks are performed skilfully. Our thinking can be impetuous, reaching decisions or acting before giving proper consideration to the problem or situation (what is already known about the problem or situation, such as, what led to it? why is a decision or action necessary at this time?), the possibilities that it presents (which opportunities arise? which issues are important to consider?) and the possible effects of different actions. At other times, our thinking can be biased because we are not sufficiently self-critical about our own thinking processes and opinions, and we do not actively seek out alternative viewpoints to our own. There are many other such examples of where thinking can go wrong. Sylwester recognises the potential of experience and instruction to make our brains faster and more efficient:

> the idea that aspects of thinking may be inherent in the structure of our brains is not an argument against bringing these processes to consciousness and practising to improve them. Thinking skills probably emerge like the structure of language – which we master unconsciously before we consciously understand it.
> (Brandt 2001: p.173)

Teaching thinking is therefore taken to mean in this book (and more widely, in the research literature) *guiding and supporting pupils to improve the quality of their thinking, thus enabling them to perform thinking tasks more skilfully*. Mathew Lipman (2003: p.263) puts it very well when he argues that education is not the extraction of a reasonable adult out of an unreasonable child, but a development of the child's impulses to be reasonable.

In what kind of directions might we look for improvements in pupils' thinking and reasoning? Two examples are pupils being able to think more *insightfully* or *creatively* about the subject matter in hand.

Thinking point 2
1   Which *qualitative* improvements do you most often seek in your pupils' thinking?
2   Does your list agree with a colleague's list?

Which thinking skills can be developed within the school curriculum?

One thing that we need to be clear about from the outset is the scale of the enterprise that is embarked upon when teaching thinking. To illustrate this, I shall quote from Lipman who has written extensively on the theme of teaching thinking skills to children:

> 'Thinking skills' is a catchall phrase. It ranges from very specific to very general abilities, from proficiency in logical reasoning to the witty perception of remote resemblances, from the capacity to decompose a whole into parts to the capacity to assemble random words or things to make them well-fitting parts of a whole, the ability to explain how a situation may have come about to the ability to foretell how a process will likely eventuate, from a proficiency in discerning uniformities and similarities to a proficiency in noting dissimilarities and uniqueness ... – the list is endless, because it consists of nothing less than an inventory of the intellectual powers of humankind. Insofar as each intelligent human activity is different, it involves a different assemblage of thinking skills – differently sequenced, synchronized, and orchestrated.
>
> (Lipman 2003: p.162)

Given that the list of thinking skills is, seemingly, endless, it is natural to feel despondent about the prospect of enhancing your pupils' thinking. Where to start is one of the first questions that may occur to you: which skills to focus on? Which teaching methods to use? How to motivate learners so that they are willing to expend the effort on thinking tasks is another. There are so many other priorities pressing down on teachers and pupils, especially those arising from national tests and examinations and the raising attainment agenda, that it is difficult to stay focused on the task of enhancing pupils' thinking. These important matters cannot be pushed aside. However it is worthwhile to emphasise that enhancing pupils' thinking can help schools address other important educational agendas, including raising attainment.

A very helpful starting point is to reflect on which particular thinking skills you would wish to see enhanced in your pupils. Would you choose analysis, or being able to justify an answer or point of view, or evaluation, or something else?

Thinking point 3

1   Which particular thinking skills would you wish to see enhanced in your pupils? Make a list in order of priority. Think about why you consider each thinking skill on your list to be important.

2   Does your list agree with a colleague's list, and are the reasons for including certain skills the same?

3   Ask your pupils, 'Which thinking skills are most important to help you learn?' How does your list compare with theirs?

The 5–14 national curriculum guidelines provide many examples of thinking skills which can be developed within the different curricular areas. Below are some extracts, taken from four different areas, to illustrate the important place given to developing pupils' thinking.

Extract A

pupils learn how to find out things for themselves ... learning activities encourage pupils to take responsibility for their own learning, to assess their own strengths and weaknesses and to develop an awareness of the needs of others. ... Learning and thinking skills involve creative thinking, decision-making, reasoning and problem-solving. Equally important is the ability to identify, organize and process the information required, and to access, comprehend, collate and restructure information from a variety of ICT and other resources.

Extract B

To promote pupils' cognitive development by including questioning, reasoning, problem-solving and decision-making; creative, imaginative, divergent thinking; gaining selecting and using information; developing good learning strategies; applying knowledge and understanding; evaluating the work of self and others.

To contribute to pupils' personal development by encouraging independence of thought, informed judgement and action.

Pupils learn to communicate with others and to interpret and respond to the different ways in which others communicate. Positive attitudes to others are also developed as pupils work together.

Extract C
>Providing opportunities which involve thinking, for example, speculating; hypothesizing; discovering; reflecting; generalizing; synthesizing; classifying; evaluating.

Extract D
>To understand the nature and purpose of ... To develop confidence in using and applying ..., and to learn to enjoy its challenges and aesthetic satisfactions.

Thinking point 4
Can you 'spot' which set of 5-14 guidelines each extract is taken from? Select from: English Language, Environmental Studies, Expressive Arts, Gaelic, Health Education, Information and Communications Technology, Latin, Mathematics, Modern Languages, Personal and Social Development, Religious and Moral Education.

[Note: The answers are listed at the end of the chapter.]

Many teachers – even primary teachers who are very familiar with teaching across the curriculum – don't find it easy to identify which curricular area is being referred to in each abstract! An obvious explanation for this is that teachers don't have time to re-read the documents to keep them fresh in their memories. Another possible explanation is that the thinking skills are not really visible in the way that the curriculum is presently delivered because the main focus of classroom activities is on learning facts, concepts and techniques. Or the thinking skills are generalisable and so go across many areas of the curriculum; they don't 'belong' just to the one area. We tend to associate creative thinking with the expressive arts and logical thinking and problem-solving with mathematics, and yet one can often recognise the important place of these same skills elsewhere in the curriculum.

Developing a language of thinking

Earlier, it was suggested that you might ask your pupils this question: 'Which thinking skills are most important to help you learn?'

If you tried out this suggestion, you may have discovered that some pupils struggled to find any appropriate words to describe the different types of thinking that they do. Our everyday language is full of thinking words – not just the more formal ones that one encounters in books or articles on teaching thinking or policy documents, like 'critical thinking' or 'analysis' or 'synthesis' or 'evaluation' – but commonplace words like 'wonder' or 'guess' or 'imagination'.

Perkins (2001) argues that English and other languages are rich in words which refer to different kinds of thinking, and *their frequent use in social contexts fosters the development of thinking.* However teachers may shy away from using the language of thinking for fear that it would be too challenging for pupils. Perkins argues that, to the contrary, introducing the appropriate use of such language *in context* is a powerful social mechanism for enculturating learners into the patterns of thinking of different disciplines.

Thinking point 5

The activity itself

Make a wall-chart with 'Thinking words' as the heading. Use your artistic skills (or your pupils' artistic skills) to embellish it with suitable graphics.

Explain to the class that the purpose of the chart is to record all the different kinds of thinking that go on in the classroom. From class discussion generate a few words to place on the chart. Then get pupils to listen out for other thinking words that are spoken during classroom talk, to list on the chart. You can help this process by drawing attention to the thinking words which you use. It may be that you can set this up as a group activity with each group keeping its own record of thinking words.

When new words get added to the chart explore with pupils how they are different from some other words that are already listed. Is 'imagining' like 'wondering'? Is 'idea' like 'suggestion'? Is 'guess' like 'hypothesis'? Also ask whether anyone can come up with a related word to any new word, for example, 'choice' or 'choose' might stimulate 'decision' or 'option' or 'consequence'.

Stop after a week. If you have set this up as a group activity, or if another class has been doing it too, then it is a good idea for pupils to compare lists. If the lists are combined, an even longer list should result! In this way your pupils might discover some new thinking words. Your class could decide to continue with the record, if they consider it will help them stay focused on the different types of thinking that they do in school.

Note: Some more 'technical' thinking words can be listed arising from different areas of the curriculum, such as 'prove' or 'check' in maths, 'experiment' or 'hypothesise' in science or 'evaluate' in history. For very young pupils, this activity may be done verbally.

Evaluation

How successful was the activity? Did you and your pupils enjoy it? Did it raise awareness of the different types of thinking that you do?

Making thinking visible

All of the above has the effect of making thinking more visible. Pupils are becoming more consciously aware of their own thinking processes and they are developing a rich language to describe them. Also, by bringing thinking out into the open, ideas can be shared and subjected to scrutiny. Be aware that this can be a very gradual process, and therefore do not expect instant results. The development of pupils' thinking needs to be a sustained process.

Perkins (2004) suggests another way of making thinking visible. Asking key questions of the class or while individuals or groups are working on tasks is a useful tactic, such as showing the class a picture of a natural phenomenon and asking:

'What's going on here?' 'What do you see that makes you say so?'

He suggests these questions could refer to a short poem, a satellite picture of a hurricane, to any number of things. You can tweak the questions to fit different situations, for example, referring to simple mechanical object:

'How does this object work?' 'What do you see that makes you think so?'.

When pupils are doing investigative activities, the teacher can engage pupils in explaining about cause and effect: 'So this happens. And then what happens? Why?'

Thinking point 6
Can you identify some recent situations in which you have succeeded in helping pupils to make their thinking more visible?

Other important facets of pupils' learning

Teaching thinking goes hand in hand with other important educational goals such as encouraging pupils to be active learners and to develop effective learning strategies. I use the term 'active learning' in two senses; when pupils take charge of their own learning, and when they are 'thinking actively' about the task in hand. Pupils can be thinking actively whilst reading or listening purposefully, or reflecting quietly on their own, as well as at times when they are more obviously involved in doing an activity, such as when carrying out a practical investigation.

It is difficult to imagine how one might go about teaching thinking without promoting active learning or developing in pupils a strategic approach to learning. If there is little encouragement for pupils to become active and strategic learners, they become overdependent on the teacher to do the thinking for them, and they expect the teacher to feed them with all the information they need and all the steps to be followed for any learning task. Many teachers are concerned about the fact that their pupils seem over-reliant on them and reluctant to take responsibility for their own learning. They fear that such pupils will not prosper when they leave school and go on to new situations, such as at college, university or in the workplace. On the other hand, when, for example, pupils set personal learning goals, plan an activity or assess their own performance on a task, they are being active and strategic learners.

The concept of *constructivist learning* is relevant to this discussion. This is a theory of learning which places the quest for understanding at the centre of the educational enterprise (Brooks and Brooks 2001: p.150). When presented with new information, learners seek to make sense of it, to construct their own understandings. This is contrasted with a view of learning as a rather passive or mechanical process in which the acquisition of knowledge is more or less something that *happens* to the learner rather than being something that the learner *does* or *achieves* (Phillips and Soltis 2004: p.33).

In order to construct knowledge, learners use prior knowledge to interpret new material in terms of their established knowledge and, without such connections, bits of knowledge are isolated from prior knowledge and are soon forgotten (Lowery, 2001). Research on the biological basis of thinking points to the need for learners to have 'hands on' experiences, however Lowery identifies that our educational practices don't always reflect this:

> Educators have long praised the hands-on approach to teaching, but in spite of the praise, books replace experience very early in the education process and are almost the exclusive way by which students are taught ... When not doing assignments in books, students spend time listening to teachers or responding to their questions.
>
> We can learn from books if our experiential foundation is well established. To learn geometry, we must have experience of handling geometric forms and comparing them for similarities and differences. To learn about electricity we must explore relationships among cells, wires and bulbs. To read a word on a page, we must first have a concept for the word within ourselves. The power of well-written books is that they lead us beyond direct experience and into abstractions of thought that cannot be reached directly.
>
> Expert teachers never forget that it is only by using the senses when interacting with an environment that students come to recognize patterns and learn about the world around them.
>
> (Lowery 2001: pp.179–80)

Thinking point 7
1   Can you identify some ways in which you are already encouraging your pupils to be more active, strategic learners?
2   Which other ways could you introduce?

The next *Thinking point* introduces seven important facets of the learning environment that need to be focused on, in order to promote a *thinking curriculum*. These aspects are closely interrelated, for example, active learning is an effective means to promote deep understanding:

1 Developing cognitive skills.
2 Developing learning strategies and pupils' self-knowledge as learners.
3 Promoting active learning.
4 Promoting deep understanding.
5 Attending to the emotional dimensions of thinking.
6 Attending to the social side of thinking and the social climate in the classroom.
7 Attending to pupils' willingness to learn.

From the extracts of curricular documents given earlier in this chapter, one can identify some examples of each aspect being referred to:

1 The development of cognitive skills. Examples: reasoning, evaluating.
2 The development of learning strategies and self-knowledge as a learner. Examples: evaluating one's own performance, planning.
3 Active learning. Examples: developing theories through investigation, exploring.
4 Deep understanding. Example: understanding the nature and purpose of a subject.
5 The emotional dimensions of thinking. Examples: confidence, enjoyment.
6 The social side of thinking and the social climate in the classroom. Examples: responding to the different ways in which others communicate, being able to express one's own ideas and feelings.
7 Pupils' willingness to learn. Example: young children are eager to make sense of their world.

Thinking point 8

1   Analyse extracts A to D, together with the quotation from *A Curriculum Framework for Children 3–5* given earlier in this chapter (p. 3). Using these sources, provide further examples of each of the seven aspects of the learning environment listed above.

2   Now analyse the curriculum guidelines for an area of the curriculum or a course that you teach. Can you find still further examples to place under each heading?

Practical constraints

Finally, it is vitally important to recognise the many practical constraints facing teachers and school managers when attempting to create a thinking curriculum. If the practical constraints are ignored, there is a real danger of unrealistic demands being placed on everyone, which lessens the chances of success, and results in colleagues who would otherwise be interested becoming switched off. Pupils too may feel under too much pressure to succeed at school, especially older pupils studying towards certificate examinations or in classrooms in which there is a very competitive atmosphere. Some may respond by taking a surface approach to learning, and it then becomes harder for teachers and parents to persuade them to think at a deeper level.

When one is fully aware of the constraints, one can plan realistically and perhaps discover effective ways to overcome or reduce certain hurdles. Teachers' and school managers' opinions and concerns need to be listened to by policy makers and curriculum designers at a national level in order to effect some of the changes that are necessary to create better conditions in classrooms for pupils' thinking to be enhanced. Similarly, there needs to be a proper conduit for the opinions and concerns of parents and pupils to come forward. The issue of dealing with practical constraints will be revisited in later chapters.

Thinking point 9

1   What are the constraints to developing a thinking curriculum, in your opinion? List the main ones which occur to you.
2   Engage in some conversations with other teachers, pupils, parents and school managers in order to widen your perspective on this issue.

KEY MESSAGES

1 A wide range of thinking skills is encompassed within the Scottish curriculum. Although particular skills tend to be associated with certain areas of the curriculum, such as logical thinking with mathematics, they have broader applicability across the whole curriculum and to everyday life.

2 Teaching thinking involves guiding and supporting pupils to improve the quality of their thinking, thus enabling them to perform thinking tasks more skilfully.

3 Content and process go hand-in-hand when thinking skills are blended naturally into topics. This is an infusion approach to teaching thinking. Opportunities to focus explicitly on developing particular thinking skills should be identified in advance.

4 Developing a language of thinking can help foster the development of thinking. A rich variety of words capture different aspects of thinking, such as wonder, guess or hypothesise. These should feature regularly in classroom talk.

5 Making thinking visible helps pupils become more aware of their own thinking processes. By bringing thinking out into the open, ideas can be shared and subjected to wider scrutiny.

6 For pupils' competence and confidence as thinkers to grow, a sustained approach is needed in which regular opportunities are afforded to practise a range of thinking skills.

7 The development of cognitive skills is only one, albeit important, piece of the jigsaw, when seeking to put in place a 'thinking curriculum'.

8 To create better conditions for pupils' thinking to be enhanced, the practical constraints must be recognised and addressed. Surface learning strategies can result from too narrow a focus on examination performance.

Recommended further reading

Brandt, R. (2001) On Teaching Brains to Think: A Conversation with Robert Sylwester, in Costa, A.L. (ed.) *Developing Minds: A Resource Book for Teaching Thinking (3rd edition)*. Alexandria V.A.: Association for Supervision and Curriculum Development.

This is a brief and thoughtful discussion on how emerging knowledge of brain biology can cast light on questions which interest educators concerning the development of thinking skills.

Hall, J. (2005) *Neuroscience and Education: A review of the contribution of brain science to teaching and learning*. Edinburgh: Scottish Council for Research in Education.

www.scre.ac.uk/cat/1860030904

A key finding of this review is that we must be careful to distinguish between neuroscience, psychology, and education and be cautious about how we translate findings from one area into another.

Nisbet, J. (1990) 'Teaching Thinking: an Introduction to the Research Literature' *Spotlight* No. 26 Edinburgh: The Scottish Council for Research in Education.

www.scre.ac.uk/spotlight/spotlight26

Although written in 1990, this brief summary of the main strands of thinking skills research is still highly relevant today.

Tishman, S., Perkins, D., and Jay, E. (1995) *The Thinking Classroom: Learning and Teaching in a Culture of Thinking* Needham Heights, MA: Allyn and Bacon. See Chapters 1–3.

This very readable text sets out the foundations of developing a culture of thinking in the classroom from both a theoretical and practical perspective. Chapter 1 sets the scene, and chapters 2-3 explore the topic of developing the language of thinking in the classroom.

Wilson, V. (2000) *Can thinking skills be taught? A paper for discussion*. Edinburgh: Scottish Council for Research in Education. www.scre.ac.uk/scot-research/thinking/

Wilson, V. (2000) 'Can thinking skills be taught?' *Spotlight* No. 79. Edinburgh: The Scottish Council for Research in Education. **www.scre.ac.uk/spotlight/spotlight79**

> These provide an overview of research on approaches to developing thinking skills.

Answers for 4th thinking point

A Modern Languages; B Expressive arts; C English language; D Mathematics

2 Some approaches to defining and classifying thinking skills

> In an educational context, we can see a constant relationship between caring and creative thinking. One student who does not care much about the change of seasons will paint the leaves as if they were one dull colour. Another student, more caring, and therefore more perceptive, will see leaves as gold, green, brown, red …
>
> **Matthew Lipman 2003: p.254**

This chapter addresses one of the main challenges for educators who are interested in teaching thinking, which is trying to find agreed definitions for thinking words. Because so much intensive analysis and research has been done on teaching thinking, numerous definitions can be found. It is an inter-disciplinary field, and therefore one encounters different and sometimes competing perspectives, such as those arising from different areas of education (for example, mathematics teaching, language teaching and early education), philosophy, developmental and cognitive psychology, and, increasingly, neuroscience. Finding ways to classify thinking skills and to fit them into some sort of framework allows the territory to be traversed more systematically. It helps both the learner and the teacher to see how different thinking skills can be related to each other. The definitions and frameworks which are presented in this chapter represent only a very small subset of those which are available. They have been selected carefully to illustrate important issues which need to be considered before planning a series of thinking skills lessons. The concept of developing *thinking dispositions within social contexts* broadens the focus beyond skills development.

The challenges of defining and classifying thinking skills

When one first inquires about different approaches to teaching thinking, quite a confusing picture tends to emerge. Every expert in the field seems to have his or her own way of defining thinking skills and grouping them together into categories. I shall begin with a simple illustration. Lipman (2003: pp.56–58) lists 31 characterisations of critical thinking offered by a range of experts, including the following:

1 Reasonable reflective thinking that is focused on deciding what to believe or do (Robert Ennis).
2 Thinking that helps us solve problems and make decisions (Robert Sternberg).
3 Thinking that aims to protect us from deceptions by others and from self-deception (Richard Paul).
4 The ability of thinkers to take charge, to develop intellectual standards and apply them to their own thinking (Richard Paul).
5 Thinking that comes in or may come in when we suspect something to be amiss (John McPeck).
6 The correct assessing of statements (Robert Ennis).
7 Thinking performed by those who are appropriately moved by reasons (Harvey Siegel).

Instead of examining the characteristics of critical thinking, one might look instead at the characteristics of the *critical thinker,* as Raymond Nickerson has done (Lipman 2003: pp.59–60). He identifies the critical thinker as someone who:

1 uses evidence skillfully and impartially;
2 organizes thoughts and articulates them concisely and coherently;
3 distinguishes between logically valid and invalid inferences;
4 suspends judgement in the absence of sufficient evidence to support a decision;
5 attempts to anticipate the probable consequences of alternative actions before choosing among them;
6 applies problem-solving techniques appropriately in domains other than those in which they were learned;
7 listens carefully to other people's ideas;
8 looks for unusual approaches to complex problems;
9 understands the differences among conclusions, assumptions, and hypotheses;

10 habitually questions one's own views and attempts to understand both the assumptions that are critical to those views and the implications of the views;

11 recognizes the fallibility of one's own opinions, the probability of bias in those opinions, and the danger of differentially weighting evidence according to personal preferences;

12 understands the difference between reasoning and rationalizing;

13 understands the idea of degrees of belief;

14 has a sense of the value and cost of information, knows how to seek information, and does so when it makes sense;

15 sees similarities and analogies that are not superficially apparent;

16 can learn independently and, at least equally important, has an abiding interest in doing so;

17 can structure informally represented problems in such a way that formal techniques (e.g., mathematics) can be used to solve them;

18 understands the difference between winning an argument and being right;

19 recognizes that most real-world problems have more than one possible solution and that those solutions may differ in numerous respects and may be difficult to compare using a single figure of merit;

20 can strip a verbal argument of irrelevancies and phrase it in terms of its essentials;

21 is sensitive to the differences between the validity of a belief and the intensity with which it is held;

22 can represent differing viewpoints without distortion, exaggeration, or characterization; and

23 is aware that one's understanding is always limited, often much more so than would be apparent to one with a non-inquiring mind.

Thinking point 1

1 From Lipman, which, if any, of the characterisations of *critical thinking* do you prefer, and why? If you had to come up with your own definition of critical thinking, what would it be?

2 From Nickerson, which are the most interesting characterisations of the *critical thinker*, in your opinion?

3 Which topics and learning activities would lend themselves very well to developing your pupils' critical thinking skills? Come up with some creative ideas for topics and activities.

As a second illustration of ways of characterising thinking, Edward De Bono, in his programme CoRT (this stands for Cognitive Research Trust, which is an organisation established by De Bono devoted to the teaching of thinking in schools), links information and feelings by saying that, 'Information and feeling underlie all thinking', and, 'Thinking depends on information and is strongly influenced by feeling.' By visiting www.edwdebono.com/cort/index you can find out how the CoRT programme links these two themes with a series of lessons.

If one delves into other thinking skills programmes, a different analysis is revealed. Some programmes do not attempt to link thinking and feelings at all, with the emphasis being entirely upon cognitive skills.

In De Bono's analysis, one learns about how each different skill has been conceptualised. For example, one might pose the question, what (exactly) is involved in simplifying and clarifying information? This is how these processes are explained:

> Simplification means making things more simple. Simplification is the opposite of complication. How can you put things more simply?
>
> Clarification means making things more clear. Clarification is the opposite of confusion. Are you clear about what is being said?

In practical terms, what might this mean? This is the set of operations that students are prompted to go through.

1 First of all be clear about what is being said.
2 To be clear you may have to write out each point separately.
3 Once you are clear about what is being said you can try to put it more simply.
4 Check that the simpler version does actually say the same thing as the original version.

Thinking point 2

1 Choose an article or report that, in your opinion, could do with some improving by being stated more clearly and simply. It may be an article that you are having to read for a course, or the latest policy report to have crossed your desk. Select a part of it – perhaps the introduction or a key section – and go through each of the steps opposite:

> Step 1: First of all be clear about what is being said.
> Step 2: To be clear you may have to write out each point separately.
> Step 3: Once you are clear about what is being said you can try to put it more simply.
> Step 4: Check that the simpler version does actually say the same thing as the original version.
>
> **2** Next, apply the steps to something that you personally wish to communicate to others.
> **3** Has going through the steps helped you to clarify and simplify the messages?
> **4** Try out both these exercises with your pupils, choosing suitable source material linked to their curriculum. What is your pupils' opinion on the value of going through these steps?

Let us take another example. Swartz and Parks (1994) have created a framework consisting of skills at generating ideas, skills at clarifying ideas and skills at assessing the reasonableness of ideas. Through doing this they have attempted to create a *map of the thinking domain*. Let's take their middle category, 'skills at clarifying ideas'. The authors say, 'skills of clarification involve analysis: they enhance our understanding and the ability to use information.' (1994: p.6). This is their breakdown of what clarifying ideas entails (1994: p.7):

> **CLARIFICATION AND UNDERSTANDING**
> GOAL: Deep understanding and accurate recall
> CORE SKILLS: Skills at Clarifying Ideas
>   1 Analyzing Ideas
>   Comparing and Contrasting
>   Classification/Definition
>   Parts/Whole relationship
>   Sequencing
>   2 Analysing Arguments
>   Finding reasons/Conclusions
>   Uncovering Assumptions
> REPRESENTATIVE ATTITUDES:
> We should seek clarity and use relevant information.

If we select some of these elements to examine more closely, say, *Comparing and Contrasting*, and *Classification/Definition*, below are two examples of how it is suggested that teachers might introduce these to the class:

> Comparing and Contrasting can help us better understand ideas that we are studying. When we compare and contrast, we first note similarities and differences. Then we decide which similarities and differences are important. Finally, we ask what this shows about the things we are comparing and contrasting. A statement that expresses what the similarities and differences show is called a 'conclusion'.
>
> (1994: p.108)

and

> We've been studying animals in science. In this lesson, we will classify some animals. We're going to see how different ways of classifying these animals tell us different things about them and what different purposes might be served by classifying animals in these different ways.
>
> (1994: p.155)

Thus, when examining different approaches to teaching thinking and their accompanying resources, you will certainly encounter different:

- analyses of the key components of thinking (generally a link is made to theory).
- definitions of the individual components.
- linkages being made between the individual components.
- suggestions on how to 'operationalise' the components in question.

If you discover that a programme does not explain any of these elements, it is safe to conclude that it is not a very well thought-out scheme.

Thinking point 3

Examine the teachers' notes for a thinking skills programme in use in your department, school or local authority. Discuss with colleagues:

1   Which components of thinking are taught, and why (is there a link made to theory?).
2   How each component is defined.
3   The linkages which are made between the individual components.
4   How the individual components are 'operationalised'.

Are you convinced about the soundness of the approach in the programme?

Some ways of classifying thinking skills

Higher order thinking

A common way of classifying thinking skills is to refer to them as 'lower order' or 'higher order'. A helpful comparison is with 'lower order' and 'higher order' questions. Most textbooks for student teachers contain lists of examples of lower order and higher order questions. Student teachers are advised to create a balance between the two types of question during the expository part of a lesson. Often a lower order question, once answered correctly, is followed by a higher order question. A typical example that is given is:

- Which city is the capital city of Scotland?
- Why has Edinburgh become the capital city of Scotland?

The second question is clearly of a different order from the first, unless it is answered parrot-fashion. Even among experts, there may be disagreements about the explanation. Social historians will draw on different evidence from geographers or economists in order to back their explanations.

A popular Scottish History series, edited by Sydney Wood and published by Hodder Gibson, contains many pupil activities which are designed to engage the young learner in thinking more deeply about the topic of the book and what is involved in 'doing history'. The activities contain many interesting and varied examples of higher order questions (you can also find a few lower order questions which are interspersed). Below are five of the activities from *Victorian Scotland* by Sydney Wood (1996). As you read each activity, consider which type of thinking it is intended to invoke: Is it higher order or lower order? Does it involve reasoning or interpreting or classifying or …?

A

1   We can find out about Victorian times from different sorts of evidence. How many different sorts are there here?

2   There are some special places that look after things from the past. Can you name some of these places?

3   With your teacher, plan to explore your area. What will you want to find out? Where will you go first?

B

'The Queen didn't know what Scotland was really like.'
Do you agree? Give reasons for your answer.

C

Find two sources of evidence on these pages that tell us how Victorians thought women should dress for games. What does this tell us about Victorian times? Why do you think we have different views today?

D   SORT OUT THE EVIDENCE

1   How many different sources of historical evidence can you find here? Write down a list.

2   Then write down what makes each one especially useful.

3   Now think about the problems or weaknesses each sort of evidence might have. Write down any ideas you can think of.

4   If you could only have one of these sources to find out about the past, which one would you choose? Why?

E

1   Look again at Sources 1 and 2. How much evidence of crofting life can you collect from these photographs?

2   Work in a group. You are a crofting community at the time the potato crop failed. Some of you want to leave for a big town. Some want to emigrate. Some want to stay and hope for outside help. Discuss amongst yourselves what you will do. Each person should give reasons for their choice.

3   Does this disaster remind you of present-day problems? Where? What do people do about them nowadays?

Thinking point 4
1 What, in your experience, does higher order thinking involve?
2 How would you know that you or your pupils were doing it? Ask your pupils for their opinions.
3 In what kind of situations is it called into play?

Lauren Resnick conducted an influential review of research on education and learning to think which was published in 1987. She began the summary and conclusions of the review with this statement: 'Higher order thinking is difficult to define but easy to recognise when it occurs.'

Instead of giving a concise definition, she provides instead a useful *working definition* of higher order thinking (Resnick 1987: p.3), as follows:

1 Higher order thinking is non-algorithmic. That is, the path of action is not fully specified in advance.
2 Higher order thinking tends to be complex. The total path is not 'visible' (mentally speaking) from any single vantage point.
3 Higher order thinking often yields multiple solutions, each with costs and benefits, rather than unique solutions.
4 Higher order thinking involves nuanced judgment and interpretation.
5 Higher order thinking involves the application of multiple criteria, which sometimes conflict with one another.
6 Higher order thinking often involves uncertainty. Not everything that bears on the task at hand is known.
7 Higher order thinking involves self-regulation of the thinking process. We do not recognise higher order thinking in an individual when someone else 'calls the plays' at every step.
8 Higher order thinking involves imposing meaning, finding structure in apparent disorder.
9 Higher order thinking is effortful. There is considerable mental work in the kinds of elaborations and judgements required.

Resnick's working definition places considerable emphasis on the role of higher order thinking within problem-solving or decision-making. What does it tell us about the nature of these processes? Table 2.1 sets out my analysis.

Table 2.1 Higher order thinking as it relates to skilful problem-solving and decision-making

Higher order thinking	Skilful problem-solving and decision-making
The path of action is not fully specified in advance. The total path is not 'visible' (mentally speaking) from any single vantage point.	*Strategic thinking* is involved in problem-solving and decision-making. One also needs to examine problems and decisions from many different angles. One needs to *think creatively*.
Higher order thinking often yields multiple solutions, each with costs and benefits, rather than unique solutions. It involves nuanced judgement and interpretation. It involves the application of multiple criteria, which sometimes conflict with one another.	In the real world, problem-solving and decision-making often have these characteristics. *Critical thinking* is an important element of problem-solving and decision-making.
Higher order thinking often involves uncertainty. Not everything that bears on the task at hand is known.	Problem-solving and decision-making require *persistence* in the face of uncertainty, and good *analytical skills*, in order to identify what is known or unknown about the problem or situation.
Higher order thinking involves self-regulation of the thinking process. We do not recognise higher order thinking in an individual when someone else 'calls the plays' at every step.	*Metacognition* is a key element in successful problem-solving and decision-making. Metacognition involves the learner in monitoring and regulating his or her own thinking.
Higher order thinking involves imposing meaning, finding structure in apparent disorder.	Solving a difficult problem or reaching a complex decision are *active ways* of getting to *understand* a problem or situation at a deeper level.
Higher order thinking is effortful. There is considerable mental work in the kinds of elaborations and judgements required.	It follows from this that *motivation* is an important element in problem-solving and decision-making.

Thinking point 5

1 How well does Resnick's working definition of higher order thinking capture what is involved in solving complex, real world problems? Draw on some recent experiences of your own to gauge this.

2 For teachers who are setting out to create a 'thinking curriculum', what are the main implications which arise from this definition?

A hierarchy of thinking skills

Benjamin Bloom and his colleagues are well known for their taxonomy of educational objectives which they produced in 1956. The taxonomy identifies six main categories of cognitive skills, arranged in a hierarchy, with higher order thinking at the upper levels:

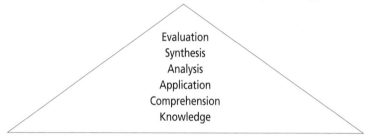

Evaluation
Synthesis
Analysis
Application
Comprehension
Knowledge

It is designed in such a way that, in order to demonstrate application, you need to be able to comprehend situations, and that in turn demands knowledge, and so on, for each level in the hierarchy. There is a list of thinking skills associated with each category. For example, *appraise*, *judge* and *criticise* are three of the skills listed under Evaluation, and *recall*, *identify* and *label* are three of the skills listed under Knowledge.

Thinking point 6

Relate each skill below to one of Bloom's categories, for example, recall with knowledge.

apply	criticize	explain	organize	summarize
appraise	decide	extrapolate	plan	translate
arrange	define	formulate	predict	understand
categorize	describe	group	produce	check
design	hypothesize	propose	classify	detect
identify	recall	collect	differentiate	infer
recognize	combine	distinguish	interpret	relate
connect	examine	judge	show	construct
experiment	label	solve		

Bloom's taxonomy is listed at the end of the chapter. Following this, other similar taxonomies have been developed, see, for example, Marzano (2001) and Presseisen (2001).

It has been argued that, while, at the time, Bloom's taxonomy may have appeared as a landmark move towards upgrading the status of higher order thinking in education, the opposite effect may have resulted because it has often been interpreted as a theory of stages in the development of children's and young adults' thinking:

> The hierarchy was to be understood as a theory of developmental stages. Children's concrete thought processes in their early years allowed them to perform little more than memory tasks, but they could ascend, stage by stage, until finally they would arrive at the adult level, the pinnacle of the entire process, the evaluation stage.
>
> The net effect was to preclude teaching critical thinking to children. Given the longitudinal, developmental interpretation, young children were not capable of monitoring their own thought, of giving reasons for their opinions, or of putting logical operations into practice.
>
> (Lipman 2003: p.40)

Similarly, Resnick and Klopfer (1989: p.3) have argued that such theories have had the effect of isolating thinking and problem-solving from the main activities of learning: 'Thinking and reasoning became not the heart of education but hoped-for capstones that many students never reached.' Cognitive research has for some time pointed towards a different view, in which higher order thinking is the hallmark of successful learning at all levels:

> Children cannot understand what they read without making inferences and using information that goes beyond what is written in the text. They cannot become good writers without engaging in complex problem solving-like processes. Basic mathematics will not be effectively learned if children only try to memorize rules for manipulating written numerical symbols. All of this implies that 'basic' and 'higher order' skills cannot be clearly separated.
>
> (Resnick, 1987, p.45)

Resnick takes this argument further by suggesting that the term 'higher order' skills is fundamentally misleading because it suggests that another set of skills, presumably called 'lower order' skills, has to come first in the teaching order.

This assumption – that there is a sequence from lower level activities that do not require much independent thinking or judgement to higher level ones that do – colors much educational theory and practice. Implicitly at least, it justifies long years of drill on the 'basics' before thinking and problem-solving are demanded. Cognitive research on the nature of basic skills such as reading and mathematics provides a fundamental challenge to this assumption. Indeed, research suggests that failure to cultivate aspects of thinking such as those listed in our working definition of higher order skills may be the source of major learning difficulties even in elementary school.

(Resnick 1987: p.8)

Thinking point 7

Do you recognise the picture painted by Resnick of long years of drill on the 'basics' before thinking and problem-solving are demanded, or is this, in your opinion, an outdated view of school education? (Think back to your own school days and compare them with the present time.)

In this book there is no underlying assumption of developmental stages of thinking. Rather the view is taken that the differences between the thinking of younger and older pupils are more of degree than of kind (see Lipman 2003: p.178). Thus, as pupils get older, they should:

- have a more richly connected knowledge base on which to draw, and more experiences to connect with when attempting to make sense of new situations;
- become more skilful at performing thinking tasks, such as the aspects which are listed in the table above under problem-solving and decision-making; and
- become more aware of the situations where particular thinking moves are called for.

Skills at generating, clarifying and assessing the reasonableness of ideas

This framework, or *mapping of the thinking domain*, created by Swartz and colleagues at the National Center for Teaching Thinking in Massachusetts, identifies three categories of cognitive skills: generating ideas, clarifying ideas, and assessing the reasonableness of ideas.

It underpins their approach to 'Infusing the Teaching of Critical and Creative Thinking into Content Instruction' (Swartz and Parks 1994). It is gradually gaining a foothold in schools across the world including Scotland, and is already well established in the USA and Australia.

Earlier in this chapter some information on the middle category – clarifying ideas – is presented. Clarifying ideas is associated with those skills which involve analysis and which enhance our understanding and the ability to use information. This is how the other two categories are expanded upon, under the headings of creative thinking and critical thinking:

CREATIVE THINKING
GOAL: Original product
CORE SKILLS:
Skills at Generating Ideas
1   Generating Possibilities
    Multiplicity of Ideas (Fluency)
    Varied Ideas (Flexibility)
    New Ideas (Originality)
    Detailed Ideas (Elaboration)
2   Creating Metaphors
    Analogy/Metaphor
REPRESENTATIVE ATTITUDES:
Unusual ideas should be considered.

CRITICAL THINKING
GOAL: Critical judgement
CORE SKILLS:
Skills at Assessing the Reasonableness of Ideas
1   Assessing Basic Information
    Accuracy of Observations
    Reliability of Sources
2   Inference
    Use of Evidence
        Causal Explanation
        Prediction
        Generalization
        Reasoning by Analogy

Deduction
Conditional Reasoning
(if...then)
REPRESENTATIVE ATTITUDES:
We should base judgements on good
reasons, we should be open-minded.

Thus teachers get a practical steer on which key thinking skills to focus on in order to develop creative thinking, skills at clarifying and understanding, and critical thinking. Exemplar lessons and classroom resources based on each area of skill have been developed and trialled. Some key principles of an infusion approach are highlighted:

- The infusion of key thinking skills into content instruction can be seen to add richness and depth into the curriculum.
- Each thinking skill can be taught, reinforced and elaborated in many teaching contexts.
- The same content material can be used to teach a different thinking skill.
- The key skills blend together for thoughtful decision-making and problem-solving.

These aspects are returned to in Chapters 4, 5 and 6. In relation to *why* the key skills of creative thinking, clarifying ideas and critical thinking blend together for thoughtful decision-making and problem-solving, Swartz and Parks explain:

> We should try to generate original solutions to problems; we should base our decisions on relevant information; and we should assess the reasonableness of each option in order to select the best one. (1994: p.6)

Thinking point 8
Look back at the list of thinking words generated from Chapter 1 in Thinking point 5. Then decide how *you* would group or classify them. What ideas do your pupils have about this?

Critical, creative and caring thinking

Mathew Lipman (2003) delineates three *modes of thinking*, as follows:

> Critical thinking
> Creative thinking
> Caring thinking

Lipman regards these modes as equally significant, interdependent, and present to varying degrees in all higher order thinking. He and his colleagues at the Institute for Advancement of Philosophy for Children (IAPC) have developed an approach to teaching thinking which is based upon creating a community of philosophical inquiry. In a community of philosophical inquiry, children learn to think for themselves through participating in a dialogue in which they must reason in order to follow what is going on. Also there is a sense of shared learning going on within the community as they are led to discover that they can use and profit from the learning experiences of others. Participating in such a community involves developing *thinking dispositions* like wondering, being critical and respecting others. All three modes of thinking can be developed within such a community.

Lipman teases out the following aspects of critical thinking from the accounts of experts in this field: critical thinking is thinking that strives to be *impartial, accurate, careful, clear, truthful, abstract, coherent, and practical* (2003: p.58).

He views the role of critical thinking as being to protect us from being coerced or brainwashed into believing what others want us to believe; it can help us decide what claims not to believe. Defined in this way, critical thinking is clearly a vital skill for all citizens to possess if we are to avoid falling prey to being manipulated, and educating for critical thinking must therefore be given a high priority in our schools.

Thus Lipman links critical thinking to making *good judgements*, arguing that while the acquisition of knowledge might still be a worthwhile educational aim, it is not nearly as worthwhile as the careful honing of the judgement with which such knowledge is to be used 2003: p.199).

In relation to *creative thinking*, Lipman identifies the following as among its characterisations:

Originality. Thinking for which there are no clear precedents.

Productivity. Productive thinking is thinking that, when applied in problematic situations, generally brings forth successful results.

Imagination. What matters is that those who explore the realms of possibility must retain as much as possible their sense of fact, just as those who explore the perceivable world must keep their imagination about them.

Independence. Creative thinkers are those who, as we say, "think for themselves".

Experimentation. Creative thinking is hypothesis-guided rather than rule-guided thinking .... Creative thinking involves a constant trying out, or testing, as well as searching for firm support ...

Expression. Creative thinking is expressive of the thinker as well as of that which is thought about.

Self-transcendence. The restlessness of creative thinking reveals itself in a striving to go beyond its previous level. (2003: p.245)

Caring thinking links thinking and feelings. It involves both thinking solicitously about the subject matter and being concerned about one's *manner* of thinking. It arises from a concern for matters of importance to the individual. Without caring, Lipman argues, thinking is devoid of a values component, and without emotion, thinking would be flat and uninteresting. For example, David in his art class uses shading in his drawings in order to create an impression of depth, and he spends lots of time experimenting with different effects to produce the best drawings he can. Laura takes time to check that she has answered every point in the question before moving onto the next one, because she is concerned to give full responses and she wants to do well in the test. Abed reflects carefully on the opinions of other members of the class because he respects them and realises that by doing so, this might help shape his thinking on the topic.

Lipman observes that in present-day classrooms, critical thinking often gets the most attention. He asserts that, if teachers emphasised creative and caring thinking more, a classroom, 'could not be a factory for the production of solely intellectual operations, wholly indifferent to or actually hostile to the consideration, respect, and appreciation that the members of the class might have for each other or the subject to be studied.' (2003: p.202).

Thinking point 9

1   Are the ways in which Lipman has characterised critical thinking and creative thinking helpful to you, as a teacher?

2   How might class members demonstrate their consideration, respect, and appreciation for each other and the subject being studied? How might teachers encourage this to happen?

3   Compare and contrast the analyses of Resnick, Bloom, Swartz and Parks, and Lipman. What are the main similarities and differences? Which conclusions do you reach about ways of defining and classifying thinking skills?

The development of thinking dispositions in social contexts

Thinking dispositions, according to David Perkins (2001), refer to trends in the way different people think. Why are they important? Perkins argues:

> The basic observation urging attention to the dispositional side of thinking is strikingly simple: In real world situations, what's important is not just what you are able to do as a thinker but what you tend to do. (Perkins 2001: p.158)

What do thinking dispositions consist of? Perkins uses the example of open-mindedness to answer this question:

> It's especially valuable to make a distinction among sensitivity, inclination and ability. ... To function in an open-minded way, Roger has to be sensitive to occasions that call for open-mindedness, such as in instances surrounding the civil rights of minority groups or the attitudes of people from different cultures. After Roger detects such a situation, he should be inclined to look at it from various viewpoints – motivated, ready to make the investment of effort. And, if so inclined, he needs to have the ability to do so. These distinctions are important because sensitivity, inclination and ability do not always go together. You can have one without the others. But to behave regularly in an open-minded way, you need all three. ... Sensitivity and inclination have to do with what challenges of thinking you detect as you go about your daily activities and what you feel you should do about them.
>
> (2001: p.158–9)

How do thinking dispositions develop? The social context matters a great deal, according to Perkins. His analysis of the influence of the social context examines abilities first, then inclination, then sensitivity:

> When all goes well people pool their abilities as they think together. Perhaps the simplest form of this is dividing up the work: You tackle this part and I'll tackle that part. But dividing up the work is only part of the story. As people discuss and argue, they pool information, experiences, and ideas to form a richer mix. They also provide critical checks on one another's thinking. The discourse also produces more metacognition – more explicit recognition of the thinking moves in play – simply because the participants need to articulate their thoughts to communicate and thus make their patterns of thinking more salient and subject to examination. Of course, efforts to join together in thinking can also be acrimonious and chaotic, but often the result is a collective process of thought more potent than any one contributor's thinking.
>
> Ability is hardly the end of the story. The social distribution of thinking has implications for how people are inclined to think. Bringing diverse views to the table tends to stimulate exploratory thinking if the discussion does not degenerate into participants taking positions. Competing views can stimulate a search for evidence. When people work together, the social interplay generates greater investment in the matter at hand.
>
> ... When people work together, any individual may detect a situation that calls for the attention of the group. The different participants, bringing with them their distinct personal histories, are likely to be sensitive to different things, thus expanding the overall alertness of the group. (2001: p.159)

Thinking point 10

1   Do you consider that it is helpful to go beyond abilities when considering the development of pupils' thinking?

2   Use this model of sensitivity, inclination and ability to analyse some recent situations in which some of your pupils have or have not succeeded with a thinking task.

3   David Perkins uses open-mindedness as an example of a thinking disposition. Which other thinking dispositions are important for your pupils to develop?

4   What is the social context like in your classroom? Is it likely to foster a range of thinking dispositions?

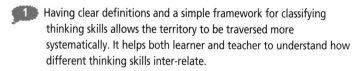

1 Having clear definitions and a simple framework for classifying thinking skills allows the territory to be traversed more systematically. It helps both learner and teacher to understand how different thinking skills inter-relate.

2 When examining different approaches to teaching thinking you will certainly encounter:
> different analyses of the key components of thinking;
> different definitions of the individual components;
> different linkages being made between them;
> different suggestions on how to 'operationalise' each.

If you discover that a programme does not explain any of these elements, it is safe to conclude that it is not very well thought-out.

3 Within Resnick's definition of higher order thinking the following elements are present: strategic, creative and critical thinking; analytical and metacognitive skills; 'real world' problem-solving and decision-making; active ways of getting to understand a problem or situation at a deeper level; and learner characteristics such as persistence and motivation.

4 Bloom and colleagues' taxonomy of educational objectives identifies six categories of cognitive skills, arranged hierarchically from lower-order to higher-order. Some common objections to this are:
> The hierarchy has often been interpreted as a theory of stages in the development of children's and young adults' thinking, and the net effect has been to preclude teaching critical thinking to children.
> It has been used to justify long years of drill on the 'basics' before thinking and problem-solving are demanded.
> It has had the effect of isolating thinking and problem-solving from the main activities of learning, whereas cognitive research points towards *higher order thinking as the hallmark of successful learning at all levels.*

5 Swartz and Parks' framework consists of skills at generating, clarifying and assessing the reasonableness of ideas (creative thinking, analysis and critical thinking). These are synthesised during decision-making or problem-solving. The framework provides teachers with a practical steer on which key thinking skills to focus on within topics.

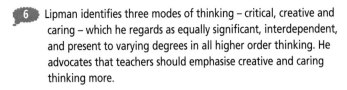

6 Lipman identifies three modes of thinking – critical, creative and caring – which he regards as equally significant, interdependent, and present to varying degrees in all higher order thinking. He advocates that teachers should emphasise creative and caring thinking more.

7 Perkins refers to trends in the way different people think as *thinking dispositions.* Two examples of thinking dispositions are being open-minded or meticulous. The social context strongly influences their development.

Recommended further reading

Lipman, M. (2003) *Thinking in Education* (2nd edition). Cambridge: Cambridge University Press. *See Chapters 1–3.*

This book is both challenging and rewarding. Mathew Lipman is a renowned professor of philosophy who has argued for thinking to be inserted at all levels of education. Chapters 1 and 2 reflect on approaches to *teaching for thinking,* with a particular emphasis on critical thinking. Chapter 3 focuses on obstacles and misconceptions. Later chapters (10-12) focus on education for critical, creative and caring thinking respectively.

Moseley, D., Baumfield, V., Higgins, S., Lin, M., Miller, J., Newton, D., Robson, S., Elliott, J., Gregson, M. (2004) *Thinking skills frameworks for post-16 learners: an evaluation.* London: Learning and Skills Research Centre.

A comprehensive academic review. Although the title refers to post-16, most of the frameworks were not devised specifically for older learners.

Perkins, D. (2001) The Social Side of Thinking, in Costa A.L. (ed.) *Developing Minds: A Resource Book for Teaching Thinking* (3rd edition). Alexandria V.A.: Association for Supervision and Curriculum Development.

An accessible article which sets thinking in its social context. It highlights the negative as well as positive forces of thinking in society.

Resnick, L.B. (1987) *Education and learning to think* Washington D.C.: National Academic Press.

A highly influential review of research conducted by a renowned scholar.

Swartz, R. J. and Parks, S. (1994). *Infusing the Teaching of Critical and Creative Thinking into Content Instruction* Pacific Grove: Critical Thinking Press & Software. *See Chapter 1.*

Chapter 1 introduces using infusion to teach thinking, and presents a breakdown of the thinking domain into critical thinking, creative thinking and skills for clarifying and understanding.

Thinking Point 6: Bloom's taxonomy (Presseisen 2001: p.48)

Knowledge: Define, recognise, recall, identify, label, understand, examine, show, collect.

Comprehension: Translate, interpret, explain, describe, summarize, extrapolate.

Application: Apply, solve, experiment, show, predict.

Analysis: Connect, relate, differentiate, classify, arrange, check, group, distinguish, organize, categorize, detect, compare, infer.

Synthesis: Produce, propose, design, plan, combine, formulate, compose, hypothesize, construct.

Evaluation: Appraise, judge, criticize, decide.

3 Using separate programmes to teach thinking

> Education has always been more generous about exposing learners to large volumes of knowledge than about teaching them the diverse skills involved in handling knowledge well ... thinking critically and creatively; and putting school knowledge to work out in what educators sometimes humbly call the "real world".
>
> **David Perkins 2004: p.14**

There is such an abundance of commercially-produced classroom resources for teaching thinking that it can create a rather confusing picture for teachers and school managers who wish to introduce thinking skills as a new element to their curriculum. The majority of these take the form of *separate programmes* which are designed to sit alongside the existing curriculum. While some are intended to be used flexibly, offering a range of ideas for thinking skills activities from which teachers can select, others are more prescriptive. Some programmes have a requirement that teachers must be trained to use them. All such resources require careful scrutiny, for example, one might seek evidence of a systematic evaluation having been done and a clear explanation of the principles which have been used to guide the design of the materials. This chapter outlines four well-established programmes. The important issue of pupils being able to transfer the skills beyond the boundaries of the programme to learning the curriculum and to everyday learning situations is explored.

What are the main approaches to teaching thinking?

Needless to say, there is no one resource or approach which is 'best' for all learners and purposes. A Scottish review of research on teaching thinking by Valerie Wilson (Wilson, 2000a) outlines the main features of a range of current programmes. You will find a brief summary at www.scre.ac.uk/spotlight/spotlight79 (Wilson, 2000b).

Carol McGuinness did an earlier review for the Department for Education and Employment in England (DfEE, 1999). For a summary of the key findings of this review see www.dfes.gov.uk/research/data/uploadfiles/RB115.

In the review by Valerie Wilson, two main approaches are identified:

- programmes
- infusion

In the earlier review by Carol McGuinness, the bottom category is subdivided as follows:

- infusion throughout the curriculum
- infusion within a particular subject area, for example, problem-solving in maths.

One can find programmes for pupils of all ages, from nursery through to secondary. The importance of raising parents' awareness of the approaches which are being used in schools is increasingly recognised. Often schools will provide short written advice for parents on useful strategies to assist their children with thinking tasks at home, or organise an 'open evening' for informing parents.

Thinking point 1

1   Download the two summaries of the reviews by Wilson and McGuinness and examine what they each have to say about the different approaches to teaching thinking.

2   How does this compare with any current initiatives in your school or department for teaching thinking?

3   Is teaching thinking part of the school development plan?

A very important criterion for weighing up the effectiveness of any thinking skills approach is the extent to which it enables pupils to *transfer* the thinking skills in question. Before launching into an examination of the key features of four well-established thinking skills programmes based on the work of Edward de Bono (parallel thinking using the six coloured hats), Reuven Feuerstein (Instrumental Enrichment), Philip Adey and Michael Shayer (Cognitive Acceleration through Science Education), and Mathew Lipman (Philosophy for Children), here is a brief introduction to some key ideas on transfer of thinking skills.

Transfer of thinking skills: some key ideas

Transfer involves putting your existing knowledge and skills to effective use in appropriate situations. David Perkins and Gavriel Salomon (2001) discuss transfer in terms of the knowledge, skills, attitudes (or other aspects such as learning styles) associated with one context reaching out to enhance learning in another. They say that transfer goes beyond ordinary learning in that the skill or knowledge in question has to travel to a new context. This makes for a 'fuzzy' border between transfer and ordinary learning since the 'gap' to be travelled along has to be seen, intuitively, as significant. Perkins and Salomon assert that their analysis of how one might teach for transfer does not depend upon drawing a perfectly sharp line between transfer and ordinary learning.

Let's examine two concrete examples of transfer which can be matched to this view. If someone is confident with and skilled at using a PC, he or she should be able to adjust to using an iMac with relative ease. In this situation, there is a small, but nevertheless (most people would agree) significant gap for the knowledge and skills to transfer across. Because the gap is small, one would describe this as an example of *near transfer*. Some transfer performances seem altogether remarkable because they represent a leap of imagination. Perkins and Salomon use Shakespeare's poetry to illustrate this:

> 'Summer's lease hath all too short a date.' Regretting the decline of summer in his Sonnet 18, Shakespeare compares it to, of all things, a lease. The world of landlords and lawyers falls into startling juxtaposition with the world of dazzling days, cumulus clouds, and warm breezes.
>
> (2001: p.370)

Thus we have two contrasting examples of transfer, one very everyday and ordinary but nevertheless important, and the other quite extraordinary. In the first example there are clear superficial resemblances between the two situations – using one computer looks and feels very much like using another – whereas in the second example there are no obvious surface resemblances between the two aspects being compared. With the second example it has been necessary to 'see through' superficial differences to deeper analogies; to abstract from one context those features which can be applied to the other. Perkins and Salomon identify two different mechanisms for transfer, as follows:

> Low-road transfer reflects the automatic triggering of well-practised routines in circumstances where there is considerable perceptual similarity to the original learning context.

> High-road transfer depends on deliberate, mindful abstraction of skill or knowledge from one context for application in another.
>
> (2001: p.373)

Thus moving from PC to iMac is an example of transfer via the 'low-road' and Shakespeare's metaphor of summer's lease is an example of transfer via the 'high-road'.

High-road transfer can occur by way of grasping a general principle which underpins performance in one area of learning, and then applying it more widely (Livingston, Soden and Kirkwood 2004: p.22). Third year pupils whom I taught learned about some of the general principles of problem-solving in the computer programming class (see Kirkwood 2000). Below Paula discusses with me one well-known problem-solving principle, 'divide and conquer', which she likes to apply widely to her learning in school:

> Paula: … you get the problem and it's like you don't have to face the whole thing at once. You can break it down into small problems, and then just take the small problem instead of the whole big thing at the one time.

> Me: Can you give me any other examples of having done that, not in the programming class, but elsewhere?

> Paula: Well if you're in say English, or in different subjects at school, and you are writing an essay or something. Instead of trying to think of what you are going to write for the whole essay, you think of what you are going to write for your opening

paragraph and then ... and at the end how you are going to summarize what you have written, instead of just saying, 'I've got an essay to do, well I can start it like that', then just rush through it. You've got it spaced out for you in little problems, how you're going to open it, just what you're going to do in the middle, how you're going to end it.

Me: Does your English teacher encourage you to do it in that way?

Paula: Yes.

Two of Paula's classmates, Scott and Bryan, set out some written advice aimed at younger pupils who were starting out on learning programming, concerning other important aspects of problem-solving. Their chosen focus was on understanding the problem and formulating a good plan before embarking on implementation:

- Read the task carefully, because it helps to know what you are going to do.
- Plan the steps in your head so that you have a clear idea of what is going on. This will also save time [later].
- Make sure your plan of action works. Write your ideas down.

Being able to recognise an important principle is no guarantee, of course, that you will be able to apply it more widely:

> In the context of programming, one might learn good problem-solving practices such as defining the problem clearly before one begins. However the formal context of programming does not look or feel very much like the tense context of a labor dispute or the excited context of hunting for a new stereo system. Accordingly, other contexts where it is important to take time in defining the problem are not so likely to reawaken in students' minds their programming experience.
> (Perkins and Salomon 2001: p.374)

In the situation described above, the students' knowledge of the importance of defining the problem clearly is said to be *inert*. There are many other factors which may prevent learners from transferring thinking skills, for example:

> when students fail to interpret current events in the light of their historical knowledge, what can be said about the problems of transfer? First, there is an issue of initial learning: the skill students have learned through their study of history is not the

skill they need when they consider today's newspapers. We want them to make thoughtful interpretations of current events, but they have learned to remember and retrieve knowledge on cue. We can hardly expect transfer of a performance that has not been learned in the first place!

(Perkins and Salomon 2001: p.374)

Fortunately, history teaching has moved on a great deal from the days when swotting up on the facts was the only way to pass the exam, or at least that is how it appeared to me as a school pupil! Today's pupils should succeed much better at interpreting present-day events in the light of their historical knowledge, thereby putting their knowledge and skills to good, productive use.

Returning to the two examples from my own teaching, by encouraging pupils, in an ongoing manner, to go through these four steps:

Step 1: reflect on their own processes of problem-solving
Step 2: abstract some general principles of effective problem-solving
Step 3: articulate these principles in their own words, and
Step 4: explore other contexts where these principles could be applied,

I am laying the foundations for my pupils to be able to transfer the skills and strategies more widely. This approach to fostering transfer relies upon developing pupils' *metacognitive awareness*, that is, their self-conscious awareness of their own thinking processes.

There are many complex arguments in the research literature concerning the nature of transfer, how to teach for transfer, and whether thinking skills can in fact be generalised from one context to another. This brief discussion of transfer is intended to set the scene for an exploration of the nature and importance of transfer for developing pupils' thinking, which will be continued in Chapter 4.

Thinking point 2

1   Consider the distinction between low-road and high-road transfer. Generate some examples of each in relation to some topics which your pupils are currently studying.

2   What are effective ways to foster low-road transfer and high-road transfer?

Separate programmes

A programme is usually based on an analysis of the main components in thinking, and these are taught and practised within a specially designed course which forms an additional element to the existing curriculum. With separate programmes the content is generally only a vehicle for enabling pupils to learn and apply the thinking skills in question. The content focused upon is fairly 'neutral' and is not specifically linked into the pupils' curriculum; any interesting and challenging subject matter can be used. One of the intentions behind this is to ensure that lack of relevant subject knowledge does not act as a barrier to pupils participating in the lesson, and therefore every pupil can potentially have their thinking skills enhanced. This can be illustrated through Edward De Bono's method for developing what he terms parallel thinking (De Bono 2004: p.89–106) and his CoRT programme, which was discussed in the previous chapter. Three other well-established programmes which feature in the reviews by Wilson and McGuinness are also discussed below.

Parallel thinking using De Bono's six coloured hats

In parallel thinking, all parties engage in a full, joint exploration of a subject, unlike in an argument where parties adopt opposing positions in order to make and defend a case, as occurs, for example, in our adversarial legal system. De Bono explains it this way:

> Parallel thinking is best understood in contrast to traditional argument or adversarial thinking.
> With the traditional argument or adversarial thinking each side takes a different position and then seeks to attack the other side. Each side seeks to prove that the other side is wrong. This is the type of thinking established by the Greek Gang of Three (Socrates, Plato and Aristotle) two thousand four hundred years ago.
> Adversarial thinking completely lacks a constructive, creative or design element. It was intended only to discover the 'truth' not to build anything.
> With 'parallel thinking' both sides (or all parties) are thinking in parallel in the same direction. There is co-operative and co-ordinated thinking. The direction itself can be changed in order to give a full scan of the situation. But at every moment each thinker is thinking in parallel with all the other thinkers. There does not

have to be agreement. Statements or thoughts which are indeed contradictory are not argued out but laid down in parallel. In the final stage the way forward is 'designed' from the parallel thoughts that have been laid out.'

www.edwdebono.com/debono/lateral

The metaphor of six coloured hats is used, the purpose of the hats being to align the members of the discussion so that they are all looking in the same direction at any one time. The *white hat* indicates a focus on information:

- What do we know?
- What do we need to know?
- What is missing?
- What questions should we ask?
- How might we get the information we need?

The *red hat* gives full permission for the expression of feelings, emotions and intuition without any need to give the reasons behind them, for example:

- I do not like this idea at all.
- I feel it is a waste of time.
- My intuition is that she is the right person for the job.

The *black hat* signifies 'caution' and the focus is on faults or weaknesses, what might go wrong and why something doesn't fit, for example:

- Does this fit our values?
- Does this fit our strategy and objectives?

The *yellow hat* is for considering values, benefits and how something can be done and why it should work. Using this hat people can suddenly see values in an idea that they have never seen any value in before.

The *green hat* sets aside time, space and expectation for creative effort. It asks for ideas, alternatives, possibilities and designs, for example:

- What can we do? What are the alternatives?
- Why did this happen? What are the possible explanations?

The *blue hat* is for organizing thinking by setting up the focus and constructing the outcome of the discussion. De Bono describes the role of the blue hat as being like the conductor of the orchestra. At the beginning of the discussion the blue hat is used to define the focus and purpose:

- What are we here for?
- What are we thinking about?
- What is the end goal?

Everyone takes part in giving opinions and making suggestions about this. Then the sequence of using the hats is discussed and agreed, and as the discussion unfolds the sequence is adjusted. At the end, the outcome, summary, conclusion or design is put together. If nothing has been achieved then the reasons for this can be put forward, and so the discussion continues:

- We need more information on this area, or
- There is a lack of suggestions as to the way out of this mess.

Instrumental Enrichment (IE)

This intervention programme arose from Reuven Feuerstein's pioneering work after the Second World War with socially and culturally disadvantaged Israeli adolescents. It has now been applied to a very wide range of educational settings. The fundamental assumption of the programme is that intelligence is dynamic and modifiable, not static and fixed.

The programme consists of fourteen progressively more demanding instruments (or tests) containing paper-and-pencil tasks of a more or less abstract nature. Each instrument focuses on one or two main mental operations such as comparison, analysis and spatial orientation. The pupil does not need to have a high level of prior content knowledge to achieve them. The instruments have been designed to overcome deficiencies in pupils' cognitive functioning, some of which are (according to Feuerstein's analysis):

- Blurred and sweeping perception of the environment.
- Unplanned, impulsive, and unsystematic exploratory behaviour.
- Lack of, or impaired, spatial orientation.
- Lack of, or deficient, need for precision and accuracy in data gathering.
- Lack of capacity for considering two or more sources of information at once (reflected in dealing with data in a piecemeal fashion).

- Inability to select relevant vs. non-relevant cues in defining a problem.
- Lack of, or impaired, need for pursuing logical evidence.
- Lack of, or impaired, planning behaviour.
- Lack of, or impaired, tools for communicating adequately an elaborated response.
- Trial and error responses.
- Impulsive, acting-out behaviour.

IE is based on the concept of 'mediated learning' in which the teacher leads pupils to explore problem definitions, encourages them to evaluate their strategies, helps them to develop a language for discussing their thought processes and engages them in 'bridging' exercises to encourage transfer to the mainstream curriculum. The following example should serve to illustrate the dynamic interaction that takes place between the teacher and the pupil during mediation as the pupil works on a thinking task:

Organization of Dots

Connect the dots so that the geometric figures in the first frame appear in each of the following frames. The orientation of the figures may be different from the first frame, and the figures may overlap.

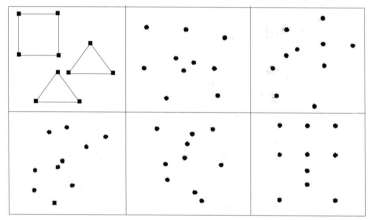

witness a student deeply engaged in a cognitive task of searching for a pattern that connects the seemingly random series of dots and listen closely to the expert intervention of the teacher-coach: 'Why did you do that?' 'What were you thinking just now?' 'How does this remind you of another problem we did, yesterday?' 'Do you have a good reason for doing what you did here? Tell me about it.' Then, shift to a classroom scene in which youngsters are asked to think about their teamwork after completing a large mural

depicting the Oregon Trail. 'What were you supposed to do?' 'What did you do well?' 'What might you change if you work together again?'
(Fogarty 2001: p.146)

In this example, the teacher has gone beyond the cognitive and into the realm of the *metacognitive* by prompting pupils to think about their thinking and learning through a process of guided reflection. The teacher can also formatively assess the pupils' learning and understanding as an integral part of the instructional process.

Feuerstein argues that it is the lack of effective mediation which leads to the underdevelopment of the child's cognitive functions and strategies for learning. Through effective mediation, this situation can be improved and the child can be turned into an independent and self-regulating learner. You can find more information about IE on the *International Center for the Enhancement of Learning Potential* website (www.icelp.org) and some examples of the tasks at www.icelp.org/asp/IE.

Courses for parents provide practical recommendations on how to improve their child's cognitive, social and emotional development through interaction during normal, daily life activities. Just as the teacher can be effective in mediating the child's learning, so too can the parents and family.

Cognitive Acceleration through Science Education (CASE)

This programme is associated with Philip Adey and Michael Sheyer. It is a structured intervention which was designed to accelerate cognitive development towards formal operational thinking in pupils aged 11–14. As a background to this, I shall quote Presseisen's brief summary of Piaget's research on the development of thinking processes as children grow intellectually (2001: p.48):

> This research assumes that children's cognitive development will follow a regular sequence, but not precisely correlated to age … youngsters first entering school are mostly 'preoperational,' or dominated by their perceptions. Gradually, and depending on the quality of their mental interactions, students develop systematic explanations or concrete rules for resolving conflicts or explaining diverse phenomena; they form conceptualizations. By their early teens, most students develop the ability to perform higher forms of cognitive operations: they learn to vary interpretations or descriptions in abstract form and to construct formal explanations of cause and effect.

Adey and Sheyer (1994) believe that teachers should be able to influence cognitive development through creating a stimulating social environment in the classroom. They describe CASE as an intervention programme which is complementary to much of normal science teaching. As such, it does not consist of an infusion methodology. How is CASE different from normal science teaching? This is explained on the CASE Network website – see www.case-network.org/index. CASE seeks to engage dynamically the pupils' thinking by challenging them and supporting them in developing thinking strategies that can be used time and time again, and in this sense it is viewed as an *intervention* to promote higher levels of thinking. It does not use conventional-looking science investigations and teaching approaches, and nor are the learning processes and teachers' roles conventional. For example, the questioning styles that teachers use within typical instruction are contrasted with those used within the CASE intervention:

> In instruction technique, the teacher's questions tend to be closed, often focusing on the checking of recall of facts or instructions, and are rapidly convergent. These types of questions usually seek to simplify, re-simplify or narrow down areas of uncertainty until closed questions indicate that learning has taken place. Students' questions rarely extend beyond those referring to task completion.

> In intervention, the notion of teacher-student and student-student mediation is central to the methodology. The establishment of cognitive conflict means what it says and the question strategy here is to maintain it rather than help it go away. This requires a questioning strategy that is open, challenging in a supportive way, and flexible.

Also a CASE lesson is different from 'discovery' learning:

> This is not 'discovery' learning where the teacher tries to elicit the 'correct' explanation. The teacher's role in metacognition is to help students to articulate the type of thinking that has been used to solve a particular problem and to identify 'why' a particular strategy was used and 'how' such a strategy could be utilised in the future.

A set of progressive activities targets aspects of formal operational thinking applied to scientific contexts. These activities are used to replace regular science lessons at the rate of one every two weeks over a two-year period. This is intended to create fewer problems for school timetabling than would occur with an entirely free-standing thinking skills programme which was not linked into any specific area of the curriculum. Pupils are encouraged to move from concrete examples to abstract generalisations and they encounter aspects (or schema) such as the control and exclusion of variables, ratio and proportionality, compensation and equilibrium, probability, correlation, and formal modelling. An important preparatory stage for each activity is the provision of vocabulary and clarification of the terms of the problem, which is described as concrete preparation.

Much time is allowed for pupils to work together in groups to explore ideas, with the teacher mediating in this learning process, and sufficient time is allowed at the end for pupils to report back to the whole group and explore ideas further in whole group discussion. The benefits of using discussion amongst pupils are seen to be:

- Providing an essential opportunity for extending and reinforcing the range of strategies needed to perform the tasks.
- Providing the chance to realise many alternative ways of proceeding with any one task and to think about the nature of the outcomes.
- Allowing for social interaction and the development and honing of concepts, events and ideas.
- Allowing for reflection and giving the opportunity for the pupil to 'think about their thinking' and share this with another.
- Allowing the pupil to appreciate that mistakes can be overcome.
- Highlighting that different interpretations can be placed on events/ideas/happenings/outcomes depending on one's perceptions and prior experiences.

Like IE, extensive use is made of bridging, in which new thinking is related to other examples in science and in the everyday world. Pupils might relate back to something similar or apply the same process to different situations and contexts, for example:

- Can you think of a time when we have done something similar? What?
- What similar problems to this have you come across?
- When/where else might this be a useful way of doing something?

An example of a CASE activity on the theme of variables, values and relationships is shown as Figure 03.02 and involves the following:

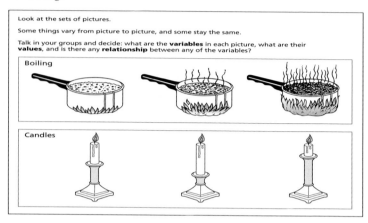

Variables, values and relationships – an example of a CASE activity

The Teacher's Guide directs the teacher to:
Now give out the 'relationship' Workcard 1. Pupils can work in groups of three or four if they have been in pairs up to this point. For each picture they should determine:

- What are the variables? (What are the things that vary?)
- What are the values of each variable?
- Is there a relationship between the variables? And if so, what sort of relationship?

Relationships can be described as 'they go up together', or, 'one goes up while the other goes down'. Go around the class to deter wrong strategies. Some possible answers are given below, although there are plenty of correct alternatives. (*Allow five minutes plus*).

Answers to *Workcard*

Boiling	The higher the flame, the more bubbles
Candles	The taller the candle, the shorter the holder
Eggs	No relationship between egg size and spoon size
Sausages	The more sausages, the smaller they are
Flowers	The more clouds, the fewer flowers

Parallel versions of CASE have been developed in mathematics and technology, and the approach has been extended to pupils aged 5–15.

On the GTC for England website you will find a more detailed discussion of CASE – see www.gtce.org.uk/research/ raisestudy.asp. You will find on the website reference to Adey and Sheyer's conclusion, arising from evaluations of CASE, that:

- there is a long-term effect, three years after the end of the intervention;
- there is a transfer effect from science into other subjects.

Philosophy for Children

This is associated with Mathew Lipman. The Philosophy for Children programme seeks to harness children's natural inclination to be philosophers by building communities of philosophical inquiry in which children learn to think for themselves. He stresses how important it is for pupils to have something worthwhile to think and talk *about* and for them to be able to discuss their own ideas. He argues that if we want children to grow up as reflective adults, then we should encourage them to be reflective children. At the Institute for Advancement of Philosophy for Children (IAPC) at Montclair State University, curriculum materials have been developed for engaging young people from pre-school through high school in philosophical inquiry – see www.cehs.montclair.edu/academic/iapc.

According to Lipman (2003), a community of inquiry is characterised by dialogue that is disciplined by logic, in which one must reason in order to follow what is going on. When a classroom has been converted into a community of inquiry, the moves that are made to follow the argument where it leads are logical moves:

> The discovery of a piece of evidence throws light on the nature of the further evidence that is now needed. The disclosure of a claim makes it necessary to discover the reasons for that claim. … A contention that several things are different demands that the question be raised of how they are to be distinguished. (2003: p.92)

Also there is a sense of shared learning going on within the community, and pupils are led to discover that they can use and profit from the learning experiences of others. Lipman remarks on how this often appears to be little understood by pupils, from his observations of actual classroom experience:

It is not unusual to find college students who stop listening when one of their classmates begins to speak. They cannot conceive that their peers might have experience that complements their own (in which case they have much to gain by hearing it out), corroborates their own (in which case they might be prepared to hold their own convictions more firmly), or disagrees with their own (in which case they might have to re-examine their own positions).   (2003: p.94)

Lipman explains how creating a community of inquiry involves developing *thinking dispositions*. Thinking dispositions are not themselves skills, but they represent a readiness on the learners' part to employ thinking skills. Amongst the thinking dispositions that can be fostered within a community of inquiry are:

- Wondering
- Being critical
- Respecting others
- Being inventive
- Seeking alternatives
- Being inquisitive
- Co-operating intellectually
- Feeling a need for principles, ideals, reasons and explanations
- Being imaginative
- Being appreciative
- Being consistent
- Being self-corrective, in other words, having a systematic approach to identifying where one is going wrong in one's thinking
- Caring for the tools of inquiry. (2003: p.164)

Lipman believes that in a classroom where there is intellectual cooperation and intellectual criticism, the lively demanding of reasons for opinions and explanations of puzzling events, and the quest for meanings and the exploration of alternatives, children are motivated to wonder, inquire, be critical, be inventive, and care for and love the tools and procedures of inquiry. They acquire – or perhaps reacquire – a need for principles, ideals, reasons and explanations (Lipman 1987: p.160).

Lipman sets out a detailed approach for conducting a community of *philosophical inquiry*, based around pupils reading a story together in which the fictional characters are themselves children or adolescents who are trying to figure out the laws of reasoning by, for example, finding assumptions and giving examples or counter-examples. The characters spend time thinking about thinking and about the criteria for distinguishing sound from unsound reasoning. This short passage from one of the stories gives the flavour:

> Now it's my turn. I had to wait so long for the others to tell their stories!
>
> I'll start by telling you my name. My name is Pixie. Pixie's not my real name. My real name my father and mother gave me. Pixie's the name I gave myself.
>
> How old am I? The same age you are.

Lipman explains how the teacher prompts children's questions by asking what interests them about the passage. What does it mean to take turns? What is it to be real? There is the problem of Pixie's age. Is she speaking only to one person? Does she have many ages, or is she ageless? The teaching method is both non-authoritarian and anti-doctrinal. The teacher's role is to subtly but relentlessly feed rationality into the discussion.

Thinking point 3

1 Which features do these four programmes – De Bono's 'six hats', IE, CASE and Philosophy for Children – have in common, in terms of : a) their rationale and underlying philosophy; and b) the learning and teaching approaches utilised within them?

2 Which are the most contrasting features of the programmes?

3 Which other separate programmes for teaching thinking do you know about?

4 Which, if any, of these approaches do you consider to be best suited to your pupils' learning needs?

5 What do you see as the main advantages and disadvantages of using separate programmes to teach thinking skills, compared with using infusion?

Common features of the learning and teaching approaches

Each of the four programmes stresses different aspects of developing thinking. There are, however, some common features of the recommended learning and teaching approaches that can be discerned, although they may not be present in all four programmes. You may have identified several of the following:

Structured approach

Building on a sound theoretical analysis, a structured approach has been developed. Particular aspects of thinking are clearly identified and targeted in the intervention.

Social environment

A stimulating and supportive social environment is created. A sense of community is fostered and pupils are led to discover that they can use and profit from the learning experiences of others in the group.

Shared thinking and joint inquiry are pursued

Pupils are encouraged to work together in groups to explore challenging ideas or problems, with the teacher mediating in the learning process.

Pupils are encouraged to think for themselves

Pupils need to learn to think for themselves. They must learn to express their own ideas. They must be given something worthwhile to think about.

Open questioning style

The teacher adopts an open style of questioning which is flexible and challenging in a supportive way.

Metacognition

The teacher helps pupils to articulate the type of thinking that has been used to solve a particular problem and to identify why a particular strategy was used and how it could be used in future.

Bridging

New thinking is related to other areas of the curriculum or to learning outside school, in order to foster transfer.

1 There is no single method of teaching thinking which is 'best' for all learners and purposes. A sound understanding of underlying principles should enable teachers to create or select thinking activities which are matched to pupils' learning needs.

2 Two main approaches to teaching thinking are separate programmes and infusion. An important criterion for weighing up the effectiveness of any approach is the extent to which it enables pupils to *transfer* the thinking skills in question.

3 It may be helpful when planning teaching to delineate two mechanisms for transfer – low-road (the automatic triggering of well-practised routines in circumstances where there is considerable perceptual similarity to the original learning context), and high-road (which depends on deliberate, mindful abstraction of skill or knowledge from one context for application in another).

4 Within separate programmes, any familiar, interesting or challenging subject matter can be focused on as a vehicle for enabling pupils to learn and apply the thinking skills. The subject matter need not relate to the topics that pupils are learning elsewhere in the curriculum. Therefore unless the programme emphasises learning for transfer, it may have limited impact.

Recommended further reading

Adey, P. and Sheyer, M. (1994) *Really raising standards: Cognitive intervention and academic achievement.* London: Routledge.

The theoretical foundations and research basis of CASE is explained.

De Bono, E. (2004) *How to have a beautiful mind* London: Vermillion. *See chapter 8.*

This is written for a general audience. Chapter 8 covers Parallel thinking – the six hats. Other chapters range across many different topics such as how to agree, disagree, differ, be interesting, respond, listen, emotions, feelings, and values.

Lipman, M. (2003) *Thinking in Education* (2nd edition). Cambridge: Cambridge University Press. *See Chapters 4–5.*

> Lipman focuses on communities of inquiry. Chapter 4 sets out the principles and arguments, and Chapter 5 presents a case-study of a community of inquiry approach to violence reduction.

Perkins, D. and Salomon, G. (2001) Teaching for Transfer in Costa A.L. (ed.) *Developing Minds: A Resource Book for Teaching Thinking* (3rd edition). Alexandria V.A.: Association for Supervision and Curriculum Development.

> This article is the main one that I draw on when discussing teaching for transfer. It explores theoretical ideas and classroom applications.

4 Using infusion to teach thinking

> *… it is the classroom teacher who, through day-to-day instruction, must assume the main responsibility for helping our students become better thinkers. The effort that is required to meet this goal must, therefore, be directed at effective classroom implementation.*
>
> **Robert Swartz and Sandra Parks 1994: p.3**

When using an *infused* approach to teach thinking, the thinking skills are blended into topics and lessons, thus leading to a dual emphasis on the curriculum content and the thinking skill(s) being highlighted. The intention may be that this gets applied across the whole curriculum. Alternatively, specific aspects of thinking may be targeted in relation to one area of the curriculum, such as problem-solving within mathematics. When planning infusion topics, it is necessary to identify which particular thinking skills will be targeted and how the skills will be defined, in order to ensure that each lesson has a clear focus. It is also necessary to envisage which thinking skills will be synthesised together when pupils are solving problems, doing enquiry or other activities which engage their thinking in a range of ways. A good classification system or framework can be very helpful in this regard, by pointing to the linkages between different thinking skills. This chapter explores key facets of using an infusion approach, and weighs up some of the arguments in favour or against using infusion in comparison to using separate programmes.

Infusing thinking skills across the whole curriculum

Below are three brief vignettes of infusion lessons, drawn from different areas of the curriculum, in order to give a flavour of the approach (see Swartz and Parks 1994).

Language topic – motivations of the characters in a play

The main content objective of the lesson is for pupils to analyse pivotal events in the plot in order to identify the motivations of the main character. The 'thinking skills' objective is to explore the *process of decision-making* through focusing on a key decision point involving this character. There would be several opportunities built into the topic later for pupils to examine other decision points, perhaps affecting different characters.

Following the lesson introduction, in which both the content objective and the 'thinking skills' objective have been introduced to pupils, pupils would be involved in discussing in small groups the answers to questions like:

- Why is this character faced with a decision?
- What are his or her options, and the likely consequences of each?
- How important are these consequences?
- What would be a good decision for this character to make?

After this, pupils would take time to think about their own decision making processes. They would respond to questions like:

- How did you think about what the character should do? For example, what did you think about first, second, and so on?
- Is this way of making a decision a good one to use when you're not sure what to do?
- Is it good to do this even when you feel pretty confident about your choice?
- Is it better than the way you think about your decisions now? Why?
- Can you write down a plan for making decisions to help you remember what you should think about at each stage of the process?

These two sets of questions relate to the *thinking actively* phase and *metacognitive* phase of the lesson respectively.

Art and design topic – the use and effect of cool colours in art

This might involve *comparing and contrasting* art objects, some of which use cool colours and some of which use warm colours. A spotlight would be placed on *how* to compare and contrast in a systematic way. This would involve discussing questions like:

- How are the objects similar and how are they different?
- Which similarities and differences seem important?
- Are there any patterns that can be spotted in these similarities and differences?
- What interpretation or conclusions are suggested?

After this, pupils would take time to think about the process of comparing and contrasting. They would respond to questions like:

- What did you do to compare and contrast the use of cool and warm colours? What, for example, did you think about first? Next?
- How was this different from just identifying similarities and differences?
- Is comparing and contrasting in this way helpful for making an interpretation or reaching a conclusion? How?
- How did the way you compared and contrasted the use of cool and warm colours differ from the way you usually think about colour?

Environmental studies topic – the risks and benefits of nuclear power

Which, of various information sources on the risks and benefits of nuclear power, are most likely to be accurate? This would involve learning how to *assess the reliability of sources* by asking questions such as:

- Do the authors know the subject well, or have they found out from someone else who is reliable?
- Has the information resulted from careful investigation?
- Do the authors have a reason for wanting you to believe them?

As with each of the earlier examples, this would be followed by a set of questions designed to prompt pupils' metacognitive reflections.

In each of these topics, the content area has been 'matched' to the type of thinking to be developed, as follows:

- The language topic on the motivation of a character in a play is linked to *decision-making*
- The art and design topic on the use and effect of cool colours is linked to *comparing and contrasting*
- The science topic on the risks and benefits of nuclear power is linked to *assessing the reliability of sources.*

Imagine instead that in the language topic pupils were asked to *compare and contrast* the main character's motivations at the beginning and the end of the play, or that in the science topic pupils had to engage in *decision-making* about whether the government should give approval to decommission a nuclear power station.

Thus it can be seen that the same content material can be used to teach a different thinking skill; and each thinking skill can be taught, reinforced and elaborated in many teaching contexts.

In this way, a wide range of thinking skills can, in theory, be infused across the whole curriculum.

Thinking point 1

1   Identify suitable contexts for an infusion lesson on: i) decision-making; ii) comparing and contrasting and iii) assessing the reliability of sources.

Different emphases between the approaches: teaching of thinking, teaching for thinking and infusion

Swartz and Parks (1994) explain how infusion is similar to and different from separate thinking skills programmes (which they describe as 'teaching of thinking') and methods of teaching to promote students' deep understanding of the content (which they describe as 'teaching for thinking').

- In both 'teaching of thinking' and infusion students learn how to use explicit thinking strategies, but with infusion there is no need to 'bridge' into the curriculum.

- In both 'teaching for thinking' and infusion, methods to promote deep understanding are used (e.g. higher order questioning) but infusion lessons are also characterised by direct instruction in thinking skills and processes.

The difference between infusion and 'teaching for thinking' is illustrated by an example:

> 'Why did the plague spread so rapidly in medieval Europe?' is a challenging question and unlike the question 'What were the dates of the plague in medieval Europe?' provides an opportunity for higher order thinking.
>
> This kind of questioning, however, remains content oriented. Its goal is usually to yield a deeper understanding of what is being taught. When students respond by mentioning factors like lack of sanitation or lack of medical knowledge, teachers usually ask students to elaborate those responses so that the class can develop a rich understanding of conditions that could cause such a devastating epidemic. The product (student answers), rather than the process (student thinking), is the focus in these lessons.
>
> How students arrive at their responses remains implicit. While some students may respond thoughtfully, others may respond hastily and unsystematically. Some students may not respond at all.
>   (Swartz and Parks 1994: p.9–10)

Although the distinction between 'teaching of thinking' and 'teaching for thinking' is an important one, the phrases are so similar that they can easily get confused. Therefore, since 'teaching for thinking' focuses on developing a deeper understanding through creating a 'thinking-rich' classroom environment, I use the phrase 'teaching for understanding' to denote it.

Swartz and Parks (1994) argue that teachers must take time to clarify the skilful thinking needed, in order to yield more thoughtful responses from more students. They identify the following three principles, which emerged from the 'thinking skills' movement of the 1980s in America, as providing the basic rationale for their approach:

- The more explicit the teaching of thinking is, the greater impact it will have on students.
- The more classroom instruction incorporates an atmosphere of thoughtfulness, the more open students will be to valuing good thinking.

- The more the teaching of thinking is integrated into content instruction, the more students will think about what they are learning.   (1994: p.3)

They argue that infusion is a natural way to structure content lessons:

> The curriculum is not a collection of isolated bits of information but the material that informed, literate people use to make judgements. We expect that information about nutrition should influence students' dietary habits. We expect that an understanding of American political history should affect how citizens vote. We expect that a deep understanding of a character's motivation and actions in a work of fiction should inform a discerning reader about his or her own conduct and responsibility.   (1994: p.3–4)

They also express confidence that all teachers, with guidance, can help all students to become better thinkers:

> Although textbooks and tests are changing to reflect this aim, it is the classroom teacher who, through day-to-day instruction, must assume the main responsibility for helping our students become better thinkers. The effort that is required to meet this goal must, therefore, be directed at effective classroom implementation.
>   (1994: p.3)

Returning to the thinking skills which feature in our own curriculum, we must decide whether 'infusion' is intended to go on, or 'teaching for thinking' (i.e. 'teaching for understanding'). In Chapter 2 one of the pupil activities from *Victorian Scotland* by Sydney Wood was used to illustrate the use of higher order questions:

D. Sort out the evidence
- How many different sources of historical evidence can you find here? Write down a list.
- Then write down what makes each one especially useful.
- Now think about the problems or weaknesses each sort of evidence might have. Write down any ideas you can think of.
- If you could only have one of these sources to find out about the past, which one would you choose? Why?

The main focus of the activity is to enable pupils to compare the usefulness of a range of historical sources, rather than to draw out the evidence from these sources (which many of the other pupil activities focus on). This is a very important aspect of 'doing history'. Would you say this was an example of infusion or 'teaching for thinking'? Another way of phrasing this question is to ask whether the above questions are intended to place an explicit focus, and to offer opportunities for direct instruction, on thinking skills or processes that are important for learning history?

Infusing thinking skills into a particular subject area

The nature of problem-solving in the curriculum

Problem-solving is a key element of pupils' learning experiences at school. It involves the synthesis of a range of thinking skills used purposefully in order to achieve the best solution to a problem. Even in those subjects which are not traditionally associated with problem-solving, one can still find many examples of it being done. As an illustration of this, Colin Holroyd (1989: p.24) uses an investigation in history: 'What was it like to be a servant in Victorian Glasgow?', which could be recast in an alternative wording, without distortion: 'Your problem is to think yourself into the situation of being a servant in Victorian Glasgow. What was it like to be that person?' He highlights that there is not a common language to describe problem-solving across the whole of the curriculum, and therefore some problem-solving activities are hidden under different guises, such as pursuing an investigation, following a design brief, or designing, conducting and reporting on an experiment.

According to Holroyd, when problem-solving is given an important place in syllabus documents, this can be for a variety of reasons:

1 Problem-solving is an important feature of the *paradigm* within a discipline: to be inducted into a way of knowing, one has to experience the characteristic modes of enquiry. This is what is termed an epistemological argument.
2 Problem-solving is the means by which understanding of the subject is enhanced (it is a means to an end).
3 Problem-solving is important because experience of solving a range of problems develops generalisable problem-solving skills

(it is a useful end in itself).

4 Problem-solving can make a subject seem real and challenging, and successful problem-solving is reinforcing. This is an argument about motivation.

It should be borne in mind that when problem-solving skills are infused within a particular area of the curriculum, this may *not* be to develop generalisable problem-solving skills (see (iii) above), but rather for some of the other reasons identified above, which are closely linked into the subject area. Thus, for example, pupils who have learned a general approach to 'sorting out the evidence' in the context of *Victorian Scotland* could apply this knowledge to learning about Scotland and the Second World War, and beyond this (hopefully) to examining news coverage of wars that are happening today. But some pupils may not have learned how to apply the skills and strategies involved in 'sorting out the evidence' to a science experiment or debate on an environmental or moral issue.

An example from mathematics of infusing problem-solving into content instruction

George Polya has for over half a century had a major influence on the development of approaches to teaching problem-solving within mathematics (e.g. Schoenfeld 1985; 1989). As other educators sought out applications of his ideas within their own fields, the influence of his ideas has spread. Polya seems to capture the very essence of what it is like to solve a problem successfully, and he discusses the opportunities that this affords to teachers:

> A great discovery solves a great problem but there is a grain of discovery in the solution of any problem. Your problem may be modest; but if it challenges your curiosity and brings into play your inventive faculties, and if you solve it by your own means, you may experience the tension and enjoy the triumph of discovery. Such experiences at a susceptible age may create a taste for mental work and leave their imprint on mind and character for a lifetime.

> Thus, a teacher of mathematics has a great opportunity. If he fills his allotted time with drilling his students in routine operations he kills their interest, hampers their intellectual development, and misuses his opportunity. But if he challenges the curiosity of his students by setting them problems proportionate to their knowledge, and helps them to solve their problems with

stimulating questions, he may give them a taste for, and some means of, independent thinking.

(1948: p.v)

Polya then provides a simple framework for tackling problems which splits into four phases:

first you have to *understand the problem*
second you have to *devise a plan*
third you have to *carry out your plan*
fourth, you have to *examine the solution* obtained

He explains the importance of each phase, as follows:

It may happen that a student hits upon an exceptionally bright idea and jumping all preparations blurts out the solution. Such lucky ideas, of course, are most desirable, but something very undesirable and unfortunate may result if the student leaves out any of the four phases without having a good idea. The worst may happen if the student embarks upon computations or constructions without having understood the problem. It is generally useless to carry out details without having seen the main connection, or having made a sort of plan. Many mistakes can be avoided if, carrying out his plan, the student checks each step. Some of the best efforts may be lost if the student fails to re-examine and to reconsider the completed solution.

(1948: p.6)

Although there is the appearance of a linear process occurring from step 1 through to step 4, it is clear that Polya recognises the necessity of retracing one's steps when something goes wrong during the course of solving a problem. (These four steps may have different labels attached to them in other areas of the curriculum, for example, in Computing Studies, Analysis – Design – Implementation – Evaluation.)

When Polya discusses the first phase, 'understanding the problem', it gives a flavour of the manner in which he envisages that teachers would introduce a problem to the class:

It is foolish to answer a question that you do not understand. It is sad to work for an end that you do not desire. Such foolish and sad things often happen, in and out of school, but the teacher should try to prevent them from happening in his class. The student should understand the problem. But he should not only understand it, he should also desire its solution. If the student is lacking in understanding or in interest, it is not always his fault; the problem should be well chosen, not too difficult and not too easy, natural and interesting, and some time should be allowed for natural and interesting presentation.

(1948: p.6)

Having discussed each phase, Polya then lists a very wide range of problem-solving strategies (termed *heuristics*) which can usefully be applied to solving mathematical problems, many of which are taught in mathematics classrooms today, such as establishing sub-goals, working forwards, working backwards, assuming you have a solution and determining its properties, exploiting extreme cases, and so on.

Thinking point 2

1 Where does problem-solving fit into your teaching?
2 Read Polya's advice, paraphrased below, on *Giving help and asking questions* and *Imitation and practice*. How well does it correspond to your own views on teaching problem-solving?

Giving help and asking questions

The teacher should help, not too much and not too little, to give the student a reasonable share of the work. If the student is unable to do much the teacher should leave him some illusion of independent work. It is best to help the student naturally – by asking a question or indicating a step that could have occurred to the student himself – and also unobtrusively – by stating the question or suggestion generally to leave plenty for the student to do.

Often the same question or step recurs; it may be worthwhile to group questions and suggestions which are typically helpful in discussing problems with students. If the same question is repeatedly helpful, the student will be induced to ask the question by himself in a similar situation, and, through experiencing success, he will discover the right way of using it.

Imitation and practice

The teacher may have two closely related aims in view when addressing to his students a general question or suggestion – to help the student to solve the problem at hand (which adds a little to his ability to solve problems), and to develop the student's ability so that he may solve future problems by himself.

Solving problems is a practical skill, like swimming. Trying to solve problems, you have to observe and to imitate what other people do when solving problems, and finally, you learn to do problems by doing them. The teacher must therefore instil some interest for problems in the students' minds and give them plenty of opportunities for imitation and practice. When the teacher solves a problem before the class, he should dramatise his ideas a little and should put to himself the same questions that he uses when helping the students.

Separate programmes versus infusion

The issue of which is better for teaching thinking – separate programmes or infusion – is an extremely complex one. An approach which *infuses* or blends thinking skills into the curriculum has some potential advantages over a separate 'thinking skills' programme, and also some potential disadvantages, depending on how successfully it is implemented.

The vexed issue of transfer

Among some criticisms of separate programmes are that they treat thinking as an 'add-on' element to the curriculum, and the skills approach is 'reductionist' since there is much more to developing good thinking than practising skills. Those who favour infusion argue that thinking cannot and should not be separated from its context (Nisbet 1990). Perhaps the most critical issue to address when teaching thinking is *transfer*. Will pupils transfer thinking skills automatically to new learning contexts?

Before considering this question, it might be helpful to examine a few concrete examples of the kind of exercises that pupils might do on a separate programme. In Chapter 2 the CoRT programme was referred to, in relation to the broader theme of information and feelings. One of the CoRT lessons, Lesson 10: Simplification and Clarification contains this student exercise:

Each of the following sentences can be simplified (SF) and replaced by a single word. What word would you suggest?
- He always wants all he can get and then he still wants more.
- She dislikes anyone new, anything new, or any new idea.
- He keeps moving from one choice to another and then back again.
- etc.

Consider the implications when only *some* teachers in a school deliver a separate thinking skills programme, for example, as part of Personal and Social Education.

- Does the programme provide sufficient, varied opportunities for pupils to practise the skills, or is it not substantial enough?
- Does it emphasise where pupils could apply the skills to learning the curriculum and learning outside school?
- Is there consideration, at the whole school level, of how the skills can be blended into subject teaching, to enable pupils to practise applying them across a wide range of curricular contexts, extended over time?

If these aspects are not properly addressed, according to most of the research evidence it is rather optimistic to suppose that pupils will automatically transfer the thinking skills to new learning contexts. It is therefore unlikely that the programme would have a lasting impact on the quality of pupils' thinking. The research evidence points to the need for teachers to 'teach for transfer', and for pupils to 'learn for transfer'.

Even when examining learning in general, without restricting one's attention to thinking skills in particular, what kind of patterns can be observed in relation to the type of skills that do seem to transfer widely? Basic or core skills like reading, writing and using a computer to word process or retrieve information on the Internet do tend to transfer (these can be viewed as examples of low-road transfer) but is this true of everything that pupils learn in school? Every teacher can have an opinion on this. There may be some occasions when your pupils fail to recognise that they already possess the relevant knowledge and skills for getting to understand a new situation or performing a new task. In this situation we would say that pupils' knowledge and skills were *inert*. On the other hand, there may be some occasions when you are very pleasantly surprised by the interesting and novel connections that pupils make between topics or situations, especially when those topics or situations have few surface resemblances (these occasions can be viewed as examples of high-road transfer).

Thinking point 3

1   Identify some specific situations where your pupils failed, recently, to recognise that they already possessed the relevant knowledge and skills for understanding a new situation or performing a new task. Discuss these with a colleague.

2   Identify some specific situations where your pupils made interesting or novel connections between topics or situations which didn't possess many surface resemblances. Again, discuss these with a colleague.

3   How would you define transfer? Is transfer different from ordinary learning? In which ways?

4   What explanations do you have about *why* transfer of learning sometimes or often does not occur?

5   What might *teaching for transfer* look like in practice?

Using an infusion approach may help pupils to transfer thinking skills. This is because:

- Pupils should get regular opportunities, across the curriculum, to practise the skills and get specific, targeted feedback from the teacher.
- They learn to recognise which skills are useful in certain situations, since they are learning and practising them in meaningful contexts.
- Pupils should therefore develop more competence as thinkers, which improves their confidence. They begin to view themselves as capable thinkers.
- This, in turn, should make pupils better disposed towards future thinking tasks, and thus their motivation to apply the thinking skills in question is increased.

One rather pessimistic argument which can be put is that, even if wide transfer – that is, to a range of unfamiliar contexts distant from the initial context of learning – proves unattainable, with an infusion approach something worthwhile will have been achieved because pupils are learning and practising how to apply thinking skills to the subject matters we want them to learn in the first place, and this helps develop deep understanding (Resnick, 1987). This is contrasted with a situation in which pupils who have studied a separate thinking skills programme, and who have not learned to transfer the skills beyond the programme itself, have gained little benefit from it.

Avoiding teaching too narrowly

To help with transfer, there is a need for teachers to *avoid teaching too narrowly*. It is important to take time out from pursuing the content objectives of the lesson in order to place a spotlight on the thinking skills and any other important cross-cutting elements. Key concepts and general principles should be abstracted, for example, in relation to problem-solving, the general principle that one should always seek to understand the problem as fully as possible before attempting to construct a solution plan (seems obvious, but many people don't do it and go straight into thinking up solutions!). Further applications should be sought, thus 'bridging' from the original context of learning to new learning contexts.

Let's take a concrete example, one that does not look too promising on first inspection in terms of its potential for transfer. I shall continue with the mathematical theme from the earlier discussion. Pupils learn how to calculate the volume of solid objects, starting with cubes and cuboids. But how often, recently, have you found yourself getting your calculator out to work out the volume of a sphere? If your answer is the same as mine, it doesn't seem like very practical knowledge to possess. But let's re-examine this from a wider perspective. What else might pupils be learning as they study the topic?

- How to interpret a problem and extract the relevant information.
- How to develop a strategy for solving the problem.
- How to be careful and systematic – going through the steps in the calculation in the correct order, and checking the accuracy of each step.
- Patience and concentration – it is not a simple calculation.
- The concept of volume – how is it different from surface area, length, weight, or mass?

- Units of measurement, making an approximation.
- Using a calculator.
- Where, in the outside world, might it be necessary to calculate the volume of solid objects?

Therefore there is a range of opportunities for pupils to develop thinking and problem-solving skills, including analysis, strategic thinking, thinking creatively by exploring new concepts in relation to other concepts that are already understood, and searching out examples of practical applications. There is the possibility too for *thinking dispositions* (or *habits of mind*) to develop, such as being systematic and precise. However these opportunities will probably be passed over if the teaching is too rushed, or if the treatment of the topic is restricted to pupils doing routine exercises, like substituting given values into the formula. This is not to suggest that doing routine exercises has no place in school learning, but rather that pupils also need regular exposure to learning experiences which stretch them in new directions.

Can you remember the formula for the volume of a sphere or how to round off the answer to three significant figures? (This question may cause some readers to shudder, for which I apologise!) Transfer involves putting your knowledge and skills to use in appropriate situations. If there aren't such situations or opportunities around, retention will be poorer. This points to the need for *reinforcement of thinking skills* as an aspect which is built into curricular planning.

Thinking point 4

1   Take a short topic or activity which your pupils have finished recently. Analyse which elements of pupils' learning might transfer.

2   How might you teach the topic or activity in a manner which increases the prospect of this happening?

3   Consider how you could investigate whether pupils were able to transfer these elements to new learning situations.

4   Do you agree with the general argument concerning how infusion across the curriculum can help with transfer of thinking skills, and the need to avoid teaching too narrowly?

Which difficulties might teachers face with using infusion?

So far, I have stressed the potential benefits of using infusion. However all teachers have experienced the pitfalls of using infused methods.

Thinking point 5

What, in your experience, are some of the pitfalls of using infusion to inject core skills such as literacy, numeracy, ICT, citizenship or thinking skills into the curriculum?

Recognising good opportunities

To begin with, many teachers find that it is difficult to envisage how certain thinking skills or processes (such as compare and contrast) can be emphasised within their existing teaching plans, and the specific matching of a thinking skill or process to a lesson or topic requires considerable thought and planning. Once introduced, the skills must then be reinforced, which for most teachers requires a systematic planning process. According to Carol McGuinness (2000) who has extensive experience of working with Northern Ireland teachers on designing and evaluating infusion lessons, part of the problem relates to sharpening teachers' understanding of the thinking skills in question. *Sharing practice* with colleagues or being involved in *collaborative developments* can provide some much needed support and inspiration, and an opportunity to extend one's understanding.

Also, what if you are attempting to infuse not only thinking skills, but ICT and literacy skills, into the curriculum? Then it all gets rather complicated, perhaps too complicated. It may be sufficient to focus explicitly on just one aspect at a time, or perhaps on some occasions to focus on the content of the lesson alone.

Striking a balance

One of the most difficult aspects of infusion is attempting to strike an appropriate balance between the lesson content, and the aspect(s) being infused. Trying to keep the twin perspectives of thinking skill and content objectives simultaneously in view can be hard (McGuinness, 2000). This can be illustrated by a brief online conversation following a first attempt at an infusion lesson by a course participant on the Chartered Teacher programme:

> I'm leaning towards the separate teaching of 'thinking skills' and their later application across the curriculum at the moment. Teaching everything at once seems to be quite demanding on teacher and pupil.
>
> In a recent S1 science lesson 'How do we tell if something is an element or a compound?' (structured using a decision-making graphical organiser) there was a good outcome, definitely more thinking involved, but a feeling that it could have been easier if the technique had been previously encountered.
>
> Overall I felt that the subject had been covered in less depth despite the degree of mental processing involved.
>
> Anne [course participant]

> Would you consider, with the same S1 class, choosing a different topic or lesson but giving them another attempt at using the decision-making graphical organiser? It would be interesting to know if, second time round, it made it any easier for either you or the pupils. Margaret [tutor]

> Thanks for the reply – there were no specific difficulties as such, only that it proved to be challenging to introduce and integrate the thinking skill/ graphical organizer within a 30-minute time period while at the same time covering the desired volume of course content.
>
> Anne

The content might swamp the thinking skill, so that pupils are barely aware of any explicit focus being placed on it, or the thinking skill might swamp the content, so that pupils are barely aware of the content themes of the lesson. In relation to the English Language topic mentioned earlier, if nine-tenths of the lesson is spent on analysing the motivations of the main character, and only one-tenth on examining the process of reaching good decisions, then very little will be learned about the latter. On the other hand, if the reverse situation occurs and nine-tenths of the lesson is spent on examining the process of reaching good decisions, pupils may lose the thread of the plot and then lose interest in the play entirely. Teachers need to be able to make a judgement about the right balance to be struck during any particular lesson. Those who favour separate programmes argue that the problem of attempting to strike an appropriate balance between content and thinking skill objectives is reduced or removed, because with separate programmes the content is generally selected to be already familiar to the pupils (as the exercise from the CoRT lesson illustrates) and it is not a key focus of the lesson.

Pressure for coverage

A major concern of teachers (perhaps *the* major concern) is pressure for coverage of the syllabus. As Chapter 1 highlights, the school curriculum from 3–18 has a built-in expectation that pupils' thinking skills should be focused on and developed. Indeed, as we have discovered, the *content* of most syllabuses includes thinking skills like analysis or evaluation. This can cause some confusion when attempting to design infusion lessons, since the 'content' theme and 'thinking skills' theme could be one and the same, that is, the content focus of the lesson is on the thinking skill itself; pupils are thinking about thinking.

Running a separate thinking skills programme means squeezing up the rest of the curriculum or taking something else out to make room for it. With infusion, the question which teachers frequently ask is how much time can be safely 'borrowed' from covering the content objectives of a lesson in order to put more emphasis on the direct teaching of thinking and to allow sufficient opportunities for pupils to engage in metacognitive reflection?

This is a difficult question to answer. Clearly a sustained approach to teaching thinking is necessary, but this certainly does not imply that *every* lesson needs to be an infusion lesson, or that *every* topic needs to be an infusion topic. However time invested early on to enhance pupils' thinking should bring accelerated progress and long-term benefits for their learning. If you are not convinced about this, consider how much time you currently spend on repeating important lesson points or instructions because pupils' knowledge and skills are inert and they are unable to think insightfully about the topic.

Lack of a co-ordinated approach at the school level

Another hurdle to be overcome is when secondary teachers don't know what their colleagues are teaching in the other department across the corridor! Furthermore, returning to the issue of transfer, secondary pupils often fail to connect what they learn in one subject with what they are asked to demonstrate in another. As pupils step across the corridor, something catastrophic happens to their brains! When faced with a task that teachers could reasonably expect most pupils to be able to perform well – interpreting graphs in geography, estimating measurements in design and technology, substituting values correctly into formulae in physics, producing a well-structured report in history – some pupils act as though you have gone mad, expecting them to be able to do these things! David Perkins (2004) refers to this as the 'Bermuda Triangle' effect. This comes about partly because of the fragmentation of the secondary curriculum, but also because it is well known from cognitive research that people tend to associate new knowledge and skills with the context in which they were first encountered (see Perkins and Salomon 2001). The equivalent situation in nursery or primary schools is when teachers feel that they are a little out of touch with the curriculum for younger or older pupils, especially at the transitions between nursery and primary or primary and secondary. Teachers sharing their knowledge of the curriculum and planning together could help develop a *consistent* and more *sustained* approach to teaching thinking.

Thinking point 6

Consider the three approaches identified in the review of teaching thinking by Carol McGuinness:

- Programmes
- Infusion throughout the curriculum
- Infusion within a particular subject area.

Which of these are going on in your school? In the light of the discussion in this and the previous chapters, how effective are these approaches, in your opinion? Is teaching thinking part of your school's development plan?

KEY MESSAGES

1 With an infusion approach there is more opportunity for pupils to practise thinking skills and get teacher feedback, and to recognise which skills are useful in which situations.

2 It can be challenging for teachers to match particular thinking skills to lessons, and to strike an appropriate balance between lesson content and thinking skills. Not *every* lesson need be an infusion lesson.

3 By avoiding teaching narrowly, transfer of thinking skills across the curriculum can be fostered. Teachers sharing their knowledge of the curriculum and engaging in joint planning will help develop a sustained and consistent approach to teaching thinking.

Recommended further reading

McGuinness, C. (2000). 'ACTS: A Methodology for teaching thinking across the curriculum', *Teaching Thinking*, 2, pp.1–12. **www.sustainablethinkingclassrooms.qub.ac.uk/pubs**

This article describes the development of an infusion methodology in Northern Ireland classrooms. It provides a clear account of the rationale, classroom methods and ways in which teachers collaborated together. The evaluation reflects the teachers' perspectives.

Perkins, D. (2004) 'Knowledge Alive', *Educational Leadership*, 62(1), pp.14–19.

This article discusses a range of relevant themes. Its central argument is: 'Schools need to spend less time exposing students to large volumes of knowledge, and more time teaching them the knowledge arts.' Find out what Perkins means by the knowledge arts!

5 Exploring the nature of thinking tasks

> ❝ Be adventurous! Choose a thinking dimension that appeals to you and design a lesson around it. Nothing can go seriously wrong ... Acknowledge that some degree of preliminary uncertainty is unavoidable and look forward to learning as you go. ❞
> **Shari Tishman, David Perkins and Eileen Jay**
> **1995: p.199**

This and the following chapter have a very practical focus on the design features and implementation of thinking tasks and infusion lessons. The exemplars demonstrate how the main principles of teaching thinking can be put into practice. In all cases it is assumed that the particular thinking skills are being applied to learning the curriculum, rather than being taught within a separate programme. Also it is assumed that the process of thinking is explicitly focused on during the activity or lesson, in keeping with an infusion approach. The exemplars relate to the work of different research teams, which will enable you to experiment with the approaches in order to establish which are more suited for your pupils. They include problem-solving activities and games. Although there is a fun element, all can be used purposefully to enhance thinking and contribute meaningfully towards learning the content of the curriculum. The important role of questioning to engage thinking, support problem-solving and generate good dialogue is explored, and three key teaching strategies for improving pupils' capacity to think strategically and well are highlighted.

Increasing the scope in the present curriculum to develop thinking

A key issue is whether there is sufficient *scope* across the curriculum for pupils to develop a broad range of thinking skills and to learn to integrate them while engaging in meaningful activities, such as solving problems, inquiring into issues or topics, and creating artefacts like drawings, personal writing or models. Implicit in this is the need to place an *explicit focus* on the type(s) of thinking being performed, and to adopt a *sustained approach* which offers regular opportunities for skills to be practised and integrated.

As highlighted in the first chapter, there is clearly a high priority attached to enhancing thinking within our curriculum guidelines and certificate courses for pupils at all stages. However the reality as experienced by teachers and pupils may be rather different! If it is a struggle to get through the content, because there is so much of it to fit in, then there is less opportunity for teachers to devote attention to enhancing thinking. If textbooks and school resources tend to concentrate on presenting key information and lists of questions to test recall, again this limits opportunities to enhance thinking. Schools do not enjoy the freedom to reinvent the curriculum, opt out of national examinations or tests, or dispense with their current set of teaching resources. Therefore, what can be done to increase the scope that exists, in the way that the present curriculum is delivered, to enhance thinking?

Not all pupil exercises or activities count as 'thinking tasks'. Some are so routine that most pupils can carry them out satisfactorily without taxing their brains too much at all! Some may demand only *recall of information*, such as naming parts of a plant or learning a list of French vocabulary. Others may involve only *repetition of a known procedure*, such as plotting points on a climate graph or weighing the ingredients for a pancake recipe.

A thinking task is essentially one which asks pupils to *use* their existing knowledge in order to generate new knowledge – to come up with a good example, generate a set of options when a decision has to be taken, predict the outcome of an experiment and later compare this with the actual outcome, make a good plan, evaluate their solution, and so on. Therefore one can contrast:

- Naming parts of a plant *with* investigating how each part of a plant contributes to its growth.
- Learning a list of French vocabulary *with* preparing a talk in French about booking into a hotel and listing the vocabulary that you might use.
- Plotting points on a graph *with* pupils choosing the most appropriate type of graph to use in order to display their

climate data, deciding on the scales to use for the axes and then drawing and labelling the graph.

- Weighing the ingredients for a pancake recipe *with* being given the problem of estimating how many to make (favourite teachers have been invited to tea or coffee with pancakes), scaling up the recipe, and then weighing the ingredients.

It is possible, in this way, to *recast* some routine exercises or activities in order to engage pupils more in higher order thinking. It is worthwhile to revisit Resnick's (1987) working definition of higher order thinking from Chapter 2, and to turn it around by considering the type of situations in which higher order thinking is *not* invoked. By doing this one can become clearer in one's own mind about what the missing ingredients are in routine activities:

Table

When higher order thinking is *not* invoked	Situation
The path of action is fully specified in advance. The total path is 'visible' (mentally speaking) from a single vantage point.	The person knows exactly which path to follow. Strategic thinking and creative thinking are not engaged.
There is a unique solution.	Following the path leads directly to the solution. There is no requirement to evaluate which solution is best. Critical thinking is not engaged.

Thinking point 1

Part A: Complete the table above to examine the situation when higher order thinking is not invoked. Is pupil motivation still an issue?

Part B: Having identified, in Chapter 1, the particular thinking skills which you would like to emphasise more in your teaching, over the coming week, and with the class's involvement, do a survey of the thinking tasks within lessons and identify the types of thinking involved.

Has the result of this small survey surprised you or your pupils?

How does the balance work out between time spent on thinking tasks and time spent on more routine activities? What opportunities do you see for recasting some routine activities to engage higher order thinking more?

There is no quick injection of thinking skills into the curriculum or miracle cures to be discovered which will turn your pupils into better thinkers overnight! A gradual approach is much to be preferred in comparison to following an over-ambitious plan or employing short-term measures. Attempting to make wholesale changes will place huge demands on you and your pupils as you each struggle to adjust to different ways of working. Infusing the teaching of thinking into the curriculum should make learning and teaching more enjoyable and profitable, not more of a chore! On the other hand, that glossy new resource containing twenty colourful thinking activities may provide a useful starting point, but that is all.

Tishman, Perkins and Jay (1995) recommend, 'Start small. Think big.' They go on to say:

> Great initiatives often fail because of unrealistic expectations early on. The classroom is a busy place. Select a thinking dimension to focus on that fits well with your other instructional goals and plan how you will incorporate it into a series of lessons. At the same time, recognise that the idea of a culture of thinking is a big, pervasive idea: if you continue to give it attention, ultimately your teaching and your classroom will be transformed in a powerful way. Start with manageable goals, but be ready to expand your efforts as new possibilities are revealed.
>
> (1995: p.198)

The need to plan for careful, ongoing evaluation

If a gradual and incremental strategy is adopted towards creating more opportunities for pupils to develop their thinking capabilities, it becomes feasible to evaluate the effectiveness of any promising, new approach in a *timely* and *focused* way. It is then possible to determine which, if any, adjustments are needed in order to make the approach more effective, and to continue with ongoing evaluation. If, having allowed adequate time for the new approach to 'bed in', the outcomes from evaluation indicate that it is not having the desired effect, and there are no other discernible benefits to pupils' learning, the need for a rethink and change of direction is clearly signalled. In this way, haphazard experimentation is avoided.

There should be sound reasons for believing that any approach being considered is *promising*. This can be ascertained in various ways:

- Identifying for yourself whether the learning and teaching principles on which the approach rests are broadly in line with current views on effective ways of enhancing thinking.
- Weighing up the appropriateness of the approach for the stage that your pupils are at in their learning.
- Scrutinising evaluation reports or academic reviews.
- Seeking the opinions of knowledgeable colleagues.

Evaluation cannot be carried out as an afterthought. The approach to evaluation needs to be worked out in advance. There is further discussion of how to assess growth in pupils' thinking and how to evaluate a thinking skills intervention in Chapter 8.

Thinking tasks can take a variety of forms

As well as varying according to the particular thinking skills which are being targeted, thinking tasks can vary considerably along a number of dimensions:

- They can vary in *scope*. The time that is needed to complete the task may be very short, such as when one pupil asks another for a quick explanation: '*What did you get as your answer for question 5? How did you get that...?*', or extended, such as when pupils develop a writing plan for a short story.
- They can vary in *complexity*. Some thinking tasks are intended to involve just a few steps, such as when nursery pupils sort a small set of objects according to their size or colour, while others involve a whole sequence of steps to be worked through, such as when each group of primary five pupils has to select an aspect of Victorian Scotland to investigate and present to other pupils.
- They can vary according to the extent to which *individual work* or *collaborative work* is involved.
- They can vary in terms of how *open-ended* or *closed* the problem is, and the degree of *structure* that is present in the way that the problem unfolds.
- The *impetus* for thinking can vary.

This degree of variability means that it should be possible to design thinking tasks for use in a wide range of teaching contexts which are suited for all pupils, since the tasks can be appropriately differentiated. Furthermore, in addition to using a planned and systematic approach, advantage should be taken of the many natural opportunities which arise in the course of normal instruction to develop pupils' thinking.

Some exemplars of thinking tasks are discussed in detail below.

Strategic thinking challenges

Since the *impetus* for thinking varies, as this table from Tishman, Perkins and Jay illustrates, *strategic thinking* is called for:

Thinking Challenge	Strategic Step (Building Block)
When you need to be clear about what you're doing or where you're going ...	STATE ... either the problem, the situation, or your goal(s)
When you need to think broadly about something ...	SEARCH ... for ideas, options, possibilities, purposes, features, assumptions, causes, effects, questions, dimensions, hypotheses, facts, or interpretations.
When you need to assess, rate or decide something ...	EVALUATE ... options, plans, ideas, theories, or things.
When you need to think about the details of something ...	ELABORATE ... possibilities, plans, options, hypotheses, or ideas.

(Tishman, Perkins and Jay 1995: p.102)

These four steps or building blocks can be used or adapted to build a *strategy* to meet virtually any thinking challenge. Through using the building blocks, pupils can learn to construct their *own* strategies for solving problems, making decisions or whatever. The approach can be developed further to identify a useful set of *tactics*, as in the third column below:

When you need to think broadly about something ...

| When you need to think broadly about something ... | SEARCH ... for ideas, options, possibilities, purposes, features, assumptions, causes, effects, questions, dimensions hypotheses, facts, or interpretations. | Brainstorm. Look for different kinds of ideas. Look at things from different points of view. Look for hidden ideas. Build on other people's ideas. Use categories to help you search. |

(Tishman et al. 1995: p.107)

Tishman, Perkins and Jay devote a chapter to presenting some pictures of the building blocks being used in the classroom. One of the pictures starts like this (for some readers this may be a sad but all too familiar picture!)

Ms. Mandly looks at the terrariums on the windowsill of her sixth-grade classroom and her heart sinks. What had begun as an exciting project now looked as if it might end in disaster. A month ago, working in groups of four, students had collected plant specimens in the woods behind the school and carefully planted them in gallon glass jugs. For the first week, students were thrilled about the project, and everyone seemed to want to take care of terrariums; there were even arguments among group members over who would get to water them. But lately terrarium care had grown inconsistent. No one was sure who was doing what, or who was responsible for what, and the terrariums were beginning to look ill. Whether it was due to overwatering, underwatering, or other factors entirely, nobody seemed to be sure. Ms. Mandly decides to take action, not just for the sake of the plants, but for the sake of her students.

(1995: p.106)

Once the students have stopped trying to pass the blame for the failing terrariums among each other, and they agree that the situation is a 'thinking challenge', Ms. Mandly engages the class in a discussion about how the building blocks can be used to deal with the problem (she directs them to look at the Thinking Challenge poster). The discussion starts out like this:

> *Rory*: We should use the search step, to search for a solution to the problem.
> *Marc*: Yeah, but we're not exactly sure what the problem is. We don't know if the plants in the terrarium are wilted because they have too much water or too little water.
> *Ms. Mandly*: Are you suggesting we also need a state step, Marc?
> *Marc*: (*After a moment of looking at the poster.*) Yes. In two ways: I think we need to state the problem and we need to state our goal.

It continues until these steps have been decided upon by the class:

Step 1: State the problem and goals
Step 2: Search for possible solutions
Step 3: Elaborate: make a plan

The following plan emerges from the discussion:

> Students go on to design a rotation schedule for each terrarium group, and, with Ms. Mandly's help, they pick a time for weekly group meetings. ... they invent a detailed checklist for the designated weekly waterer, to help track factors that might contribute to the terrarium's health, such as how much water has been given, the date of watering, the temperature of classroom, and so on. After the groups have finished devising their plans, she pairs up groups and asks each group to critique another group's plan, noting what is good about it and what might need improvement.
>
> (Tishman *et al.* 1995: pp.109–110)

It is important to bear in mind the key distinction between infusion and *teaching for thinking* (i.e. teaching for understanding) from Chapter 4. With infusion, the teacher sets out to teach the thinking skills and processes explicitly. In the example above, the building blocks of strategic thinking are focused on very explicitly during the discussion with the class. While seeking an effective solution to the problem in hand, the teacher has a long-term goal in mind of enhancing pupils' general capacity to solve problems.

By teaching thinking is meant enhancing the *quality* of pupils' thinking, and this does not come about automatically just by getting pupils to do *more* thinking. One can make an analogy with practising a musical instrument. Unless the person concentrates on *how* he or she practises, bad habits may become ingrained!

Thinking point 2

1   What value do you see in pupils learning to build a strategy for themselves, in comparison to them being given a strategy to use by the teacher or someone else?

2   Is this (the four building blocks) a promising approach to developing strategic thinking, in your opinion? Could your pupils benefit from it? If so, experiment!

An open-ended thinking task

Leat and Higgins (2002) refer to this activity in the broader context of discussing the characteristics of, 'Powerful Pedagogical Strategies', as follows:

> About eight years ago, staff involved in an initial teacher education programme offering a Postgraduate Certificate in Education (PGCE) at Newcastle University started gathering and generating generic, flexible and creative strategies for making lessons more challenging. One example of such a strategy is Odd One Out. Teachers present pupils with three ideas, either as words, pictures or symbols, such as a picture of a hen, a frog and a duck. Pupils then choose an 'odd one out' and give a reason. A typical response might be that the frog is the odd one out because it does not have feathers, or is not a bird, or is an amphibian, depending on their knowledge and understanding of classification in science ... The interest in such strategies was spurred by the fact that many postgraduate secondary trainee teachers came to adopt patterns of teaching based on teacher exposition, textbooks and worksheets. Some of the trainees found these dissatisfying ...
>
> (2002: p.72)

According to Leat and Higgins, key characteristics of powerful pedagogical strategies are that they:

- are manageable for teachers and pupils
- can be adapted to a wide spectrum of age ranges, abilities and

subject matters
- are open-ended and encourage a variety of working methods and reasoning
- encourage pupils to use what they already know to grapple with new information and scenarios
- encourage talk and
- provide a springboard to reflect upon in a class debriefing discussion which helps with developing metacognitive awareness.

A concrete example will help with exploring some of these characteristics. This is based on a demonstration of the activity to secondary student teachers by Vivienne Baumfield from the *Centre for Learning and Teaching* at Newcastle University, see www.ncl.ac.uk/ecls/research/education/li/.

Odd One Out

Over the next day or two, show the pictures below to some colleagues, friends, pupils or family members, and ask them which picture is the odd one out, and why:

Did anyone respond with an exasperated voice (I'm thinking here of my son!) – 'It's the hyena, obviously. The lion and leopard belong to the big cat family and the hyena doesn't!'. So, that was the problem solved. Or was it?

- 'It's the lion. The others don't have a mane', is a solution too, or,
- 'It's the lion. The other two have markings on their coats and the lion doesn't', or,

- 'It's the leopard. It lives and hunts on its own, and the others are social animals and live in packs', or,
- 'It's the leopard. It can carry the animals it kills into trees so that scavengers don't eat them. Lions and hyenas don't do that', or,
- 'It's the hyena. It is facing left and the other two animals are facing right'.

It is a very useful lesson for pupils to learn that problems can have more than one possible solution. Indeed, one of the characteristics of the critical thinker is someone who, 'recognizes that most real-world problems have more than one possible solution and that those solutions may differ in numerous respects and may be difficult to compare ...' (see Chapter 2, p. 24). *Odd one out* is an example of an open-ended problem, for which:

- there is more than one possible solution, and,
- for any given solution, there may be several solution paths.

The open-ended nature of the problem makes it adaptable for use in many different teaching situations including with mixed-ability classes.

Through interactive discussion *during* the activity, pupils develop an awareness of the diversity of solutions to the problem. Through conducting a review *after* the activity, interesting aspects of the problem itself, pupils' responses, and how pupils interacted with each other during the activity can be drawn out. Some useful questions are:

- How did you think about the problem?
- Which new aspects of the topic did you learn about?
- Which aspects would you like to continue to learn more about or explore further?
- Which questions do you still have about the topic?
- Did you contribute well in class/in your group? How did you contribute?
- What was different about this problem in comparison to some others that you have examined recently?
- What was difficult about it? What was easy?
- Was it interesting?

These questions have a *metacognitive* focus since they are designed to engage pupils in reflecting on and evaluating their own thinking.

Thinking point 3

1   How would you characterise the problems which pupils study in your class? Are they open-ended or closed? Why do you think this is?

2   Find out the pattern in other subjects (if you are a secondary teacher) or with different age-groups (if you are a nursery or primary teacher).

There are several other interesting features of this activity which arise from the class or group discussion. The activity should assist pupils to develop:

A A deeper *knowledge and understanding* of the topic, because:
- knowledge is pooled when discussing, therefore pupils have the opportunity to learn from each other;
- it serves as a diagnostic tool to enable the teacher to gauge pupils' prior knowledge of the topic and to build on this;
- it serves as a launch-pad for exploring unfamiliar or interesting aspects of the topic, for example, different species of animal have different social behaviours.

B A range of *thinking skills*, because pupils:
- compare and contrast each picture (what are the similarities and differences?);
- supply reasons for their response, and assess whether each other's reasons are adequate (are they valid and based accurately on the facts?); This involves critical thinking, and relevant knowledge too!
- search for other possible solutions; this involves creative thinking.

C Important *thinking dispositions*, because the teacher can guide pupils towards:
- learning to value the contributions of others and their own individual contributions to discussions, and;
- learning to challenge ideas and opinions constructively.

Thus there is the creation of a *social climate* in which pupils can feel secure about voicing their opinions and contributing their ideas. This aspect is explored further in Chapter 7.

Thinking point 4
1   Examine your present teaching plan. Where could you use *Odd One Out* to introduce a new topic or recap on a previous lesson?
2   Try it out on a few occasions.
3   What emerged from the review of the activity?

Games for thinking

Robert Fisher has written many books for teachers on ways to develop children's thinking, all of which involve pupils in discussing issues and inquiring together. The intention of *Games for Thinking* is that pupils should have fun while exercising their capacities for thinking (Fisher lists a long set of critical thinking skills which the games help to develop). The games are also designed to, 'help overcome some of the blocks to thinking, especially the three 'intelligence traps' that prevent us from making the most of our thinking – haste, narrowness and lack of focus.' (Fisher 1997: p.5).

Fisher recommends that pupils need time to think before, during and after the game, to raise and discuss questions and to review the game afterwards. He lists a set of general questions which can be posed before, during and after the game. I have listed a few below:

Questions about the game [before]
What other games do you know that are like this game? Can you give examples?
Do you know the rules? Do they make sense? Are you ready to play?
Thinking in the game [during]
What do you need to do to win, or achieve your target in the game?
What strategy or ways of playing will help you in this game?
Thinking through the game [after]
Were you successful in the game? Why, or why not?
What strategy did you use in playing the game? Was it a good strategy?   (1997: pp.7–8)

I have sketched out briefly three of the games below, the first of which can be easily linked to any curricular area, the second of which is especially suited to the language curriculum, and the third of which is especially suited to those areas of the curriculum in which pupils are given a design brief to follow (for full details see Fisher 1997: pp.21–3; 28–30 and 156–8).

Word definition game

This game is designed to encourage speed of thinking in defining words. One member of the team has a set of words. He or she has to describe or define each word to the other team members, avoiding close derivatives. The other members of the team have to guess each word. A correct guess wins a point for the team. In turn, every team member gets a different set of words to describe or define. The team with the highest score in the class wins.

After the game, it is suggested that the teacher should pose questions to get pupils to review the activity and to encourage deeper thinking:

- Do you think it is an easy or hard game? What makes it easy or hard?
- Are some words easier to define than others? Why?
- Can every word be defined?
- How could this game help you in thinking and learning?
- Do words have only one meaning or definition? Can you give an example?
- Who decides on the meaning or definition of a word?
- Can the meaning or definition of a word change? How, or why?

Poetry game

This game involves restoring order to a scrambled poem. The teacher chooses an interesting poem. It is cut up into separate lines (for a short poem) or into verses (for a long poem) for each team. The team reassembles the poem. It can then compare its poem with the original. The teams whose poem is in the nearest order to the original win the game.

Among the questions to think about afterwards are:
- Is there only one way the lines (or verses) of the poem make sense or are there different ways for the lines to be arranged and still make sense?
- Can the same words mean different things to different people? Can you give an example?

Problem-solving challenge

Pupils compete to create the best solution to a design brief within a given time. Two or more teams are given a problem which they try to solve, and they must present their solution in a drawing or design that makes their solution visible to others. A panel judges which design is best. Any intriguing design brief can be used. Among Fisher's suggestions are: a machine to cut hair; a pet's home; a device for watering plants while you are away. You will have your own ideas.

Amongst the questions for pupils to think about after the activity are the following:

- What kind of problem were you asked to solve?
- Was there only one solution or many to the problem?
- Is there ever only one answer to a problem? Can you give an example of a problem without an answer?
- Do you prefer to work out solutions to problems by yourself or with others? What problems, when and why?
- Do you think there is always a best solution to a problem?
- Is it easier to talk about a solution, or to show it in a drawing? Why is this? Can you give an example?
- Could you identify something good in every solution?
- What problem would you most like to see solved? How might it be solved?

Thinking point 5

1   Examine your present teaching plan. Choose at least one of the thinking games designed by Robert Fisher. Relate it to the curriculum.
2   Test it in the classroom. What did pupils learn?
3   The idea of developing sets of general questions for use before, during and after thinking games is extendable to any type of thinking activity. Make up your own sets of questions to fit with your teaching.

Use of questioning to engage thinking, support problem-solving and generate inquiry

The exemplars above provide a good illustration of the important role of effective teacher questioning in developing thinking and metacognition. The kind of questions listed below (we might call them *general questions*) require pupils to use their knowledge to work out a response, rather than only recall information. They serve as *prompts* for thinking:

- What do you feel are the main issues?
- What is your opinion about ...? Why do you think that?
- What would be a good next move to make?
- I wonder if there's a better way to do this ...?
- Can you explain?
- Can you give me an example?
- How does this compare with ...?
- What would happen if ...?
- How could you find out ...?

If a prompt is being used to help the pupil think through how to fix a problem or resolve a difficulty, and it proves not to be enough, the teacher can offer an additional prompt, or go further to offer a hint or suggestion, such as:

- Do you think it might be here [the teacher points] that the problem lies?
- Would it make a difference if you tried ...?

The most powerful use of general questions like these is not, however, when the teacher poses them to the pupil, but when the pupil has learned to pose general questions to him or herself, or indeed to the other pupils in his or her group. If the teacher uses such questions frequently when interacting with the class, this should help develop the habit of *self-prompting*. Instead of looking to the teacher for constant reassurance or direction, pupils have become self-directed learners. This situation would make many teachers very content with their lives at school!

While pupils are solving mathematical problems, a US researcher, Alan Schoenfeld, recommends that the teacher can actively intervene. He describes one effective technique to encourage pupils to regulate their own thinking processes, in which the teacher reserves the right to ask the following three questions at any time:

What (exactly) are you doing?
(Can you describe it to me precisely?)
Why are you doing it?
(How does it fit into the solution?)
How does it help you?
(What will you do with the outcome when you obtain it?)

(Schoenfeld 1989: p.98)

Students, he discovered, became better and better at answering these questions as the term progressed: 'When the students realise that the questions will continue, they begin to defend themselves by discussing the answers in advance.' (1989: p.98). By the end of the term, discussing the questions had become habitual. In this way, Schoenfeld has strengthened his students' problem solving and metacognitive abilities.

This approach has been used successfully with computing studies classes in Scotland. If the programs that pupils write produce wrong or unexpected results, this set of questions is posed:

What actual output [results] did the program produce?
(Can you describe it to me precisely?)
Is this the output [results] you expected to get?
(The pupil should have predicted the output but may not have done so, or may not have done so accurately. This can be put right.)
What does your program tell the computer to do?
(Leave the computer and go to your desk. Re-examine your listing of the program a step at a time, having now reminded yourself or established what is incorrect about the output that it produces.)
What changes do you need to make to your program in order to fix it?
(It is now a matter of pinpointing the errors and correcting them one by one.)
Do you need to do any further testing of the program?
(There may be other hidden errors in the program which further testing will reveal.)

This forms part of a broader strategy (see below) to maximise the opportunity for pupils to come up with most of the solution to programming problems independently (Kirkwood 2000):

When the pupil requests help with a programming problem:
• the teacher may first of all suggest that the pupil reads more

carefully or does some form of checking, e.g. *Did you check each step?*;
- the second recourse may be to prompting, e.g. *What appears to be going wrong?*;
- the third recourse may be to hinting or suggesting, e.g. *What does this instruction do?*;
- the fourth recourse may be to provide a solution and accompanying brief explanation to enable the pupil to continue with the task;
- the fifth recourse may be to provide more extended assistance, such as coaching.

The teacher uses professional judgement when applying the framework, and it is strengthened by encouraging pupils to assist each other in their learning by mirroring the teacher's questioning strategies.

In Lipman's *community of philosophical inquiry* (Lipman 2003: pp.101–2) it is the *children's questions* which are used to construct the agenda for discussion. Following the reading of a text (the text has been specially written as a stimulus for children to ask philosophical questions), the teacher and pupils co-operate in deciding where to begin the discussion. The questions serve as a map of areas which interest the children, as an index of what they consider to be important in the text, and as an expression of their cognitive needs.

Thinking point 6

1   Examine the list of general questions or prompts for thinking.

2   Which general questions do you use most frequently to prompt pupils to think more deeply, and to use their existing knowledge productively to generate new knowledge?

3   Do you see any value in grouping questions together, in the manner proposed by Schoenfeld?

4   Do your pupils self-prompt? What kind of questions do they prompt themselves with? You will need to ask your pupils about this!

Three key strategies for teaching thinking: direct instruction, modelling and metacognition

Three key teaching strategies for improving pupils' capacity to think strategically and well are direct instruction in thinking skills, the teacher modelling to pupils his or her own thinking processes, and developing pupils' metacognitive skills (Nisbet and Shucksmith, 1984). Metacognition is the process of reflecting on and evaluating one's own thinking. This is essential to good thinking because, through it, pupils can monitor and regulate their own thinking. The three strategies are often combined within a thinking activity or lesson, although all three need not be present. Questioning can play an important role in direct instruction, modelling and developing metacognition.

A key point about direct instruction in thinking skills is that any procedures must not be taught as tricks to cope with specific tasks: teaching must stress the potential for transfer rather than being mechanistic. Modelling involves the teacher sharing with pupils how his or her own learning, the task and the learning context influence performance: the purpose is not to 'beat the child over the head with a new skill', but to show how to 'select skills within the context of natural predicaments' (Nisbet and Shucksmith 1984: p.14).

Implicit in modelling is that the pupil should gradually take over control of his or her own learning. The two illustrations in the previous section of problem-solving in mathematics and computer programming (from Schoenfeld and Kirkwood respectively), show the teacher modelling his or her own thinking processes aloud to pupils. This is intended to encourage pupils to develop their own strategies for solving problems.

Likewise Ms. Mandly may have first introduced her pupils to the idea of using building blocks for strategic thinking by modelling her solution to an actual problem, one that is different from the terrarium problem, but not too dissimilar. She may have begun by thinking aloud about the problem and why it has arisen. She would combine modelling with direct instruction. Direct instruction would focus on the building blocks for strategic thinking, using the poster as a visual aid (she could either use a ready-made poster or construct it at each stage of the solution process). Again, this is intended to encourage pupils to develop their own strategies for solving problems.

When modelling a solution, the teacher should invite contributions from the class. A more genuine sense of discovery and inquiry is experienced by the class when it is clear to pupils that their ideas and suggestions have influenced the outcomes.

Thinking point 7

1   In which ways are you able to bring your own thinking out into the open when exploring a new topic, situation or problem with pupils?

2   Which natural predicaments arise in your classroom which could form an interesting and useful focus for exploration with pupils, and in which there would be opportunities for modelling your strategic thinking to the class?

KEY MESSAGES

1 'Be adventurous! Choose a thinking dimension that appeals to you and design a lesson around it. Nothing can go seriously wrong... Acknowledge that some degree of preliminary uncertainty is unavoidable and look forward to learning as you go.'

(Tishman, Perkins and Jay 1995: p.199)

2 Not all pupil exercises or activities count as 'thinking tasks', for example, some demand recall of information and others involve repetition of a known procedure. A thinking task asks pupils to make use of their existing knowledge or skills in order to generate new knowledge or skills. It is possible to recast some routine exercises or activities to engage higher order thinking more.

3 When considering how best to infuse the teaching of thinking into the curriculum, a gradual and incremental approach has clear advantages. It is more manageable, and it can be evaluated in a *timely* and *focused* way. Teachers should have *sound reasons* for believing that any approach being considered is promising.

4 Thinking tasks vary on many dimensions – the skills they target, their scope and complexity, the extent to which individual or collaborative work is involved, and the *impetus* for engaging in them. They are adaptable and generally well suited for mixed-ability teaching.

5 Pupils can learn to construct their *own* strategies for solving problems, making decisions or performing tasks.

6 Pupils can learn to pose general questions to themselves, such as, 'What else might I try?', or, 'Can I improve my solution?'. If teachers pose such questions frequently, this will greatly increase the likelihood that pupils will learn to prompt their own thinking.

7 Three key teaching strategies for improving pupils' capacity to think strategically and well are direct instruction in thinking skills, the teacher modelling to pupils his or her own thinking processes, and developing pupils' metacognitive skills.

Recommended further reading

Fisher, R. (1997) *Games for Thinking* Oxford: Nash Pollock Publishing.

Fisher, R. (1999) *First Stories for Thinking* Oxford: Nash Pollock Publishing.

These books (and others written by Fisher) contain practical ideas and classroom activities designed to promote philosophical discussion and a community of enquiry.

Kirkwood, M.J. (2000) 'Infusing higher-order thinking and learning to learn into content instruction: a case study of secondary computing studies in Scotland', *Journal of Curriculum Studies*, 32(4), pp.509–535.

The infusion approach can be applied more widely to other curricular areas.

Leat, D. and Higgins, S. (2002) 'The role of powerful pedagogical strategies in curriculum development', *The Curriculum Journal*, 13(1), pp.71–85.

This article explains more about the authors' work with teachers.

Schoenfeld, A.H. (1989) Teaching Mathematical Thinking and Problem Solving, in Resnick, L.B., Klopfer, L. E. (eds.) *Toward the Thinking Curriculum: Current Cognitive Research* Alexandria VA: Association for Supervision and Curriculum Development.

> The approach to teaching problem-solving can be applied more widely to other curricular areas.

Tishman, S., Perkins, D., and Jay, E. (1995) *The Thinking Classroom: Learning and Teaching in a Culture of Thinking* Needham Heights, MA: Allyn and Bacon. *See Chapters 8–9.*

> Chapters 8–9 explore the topic of strategic thinking and introduce the idea of Strategy Building Blocks.

6 Creating a structure for infusion lessons

> One of the main benefits of the infusion approach is that it allows teachers to examine their current lesson plans and schemes of work with the view to incorporating teaching strategies to enhance thinking skills …
>
> **ACTS II handbook by Carol McGuinness and colleagues 2003: p.20**

The main reason for sub-dividing a thinking task or infusion lesson into distinct stages or components is to enable the teacher and pupils to focus in on the types of thinking that need to be performed at each stage.

FourThought Strategy

Shari Tishman, David Perkins and Eileen Jay (1995) use the diagram in Figure 6.01 to depict the stages in their FourThought Strategy:

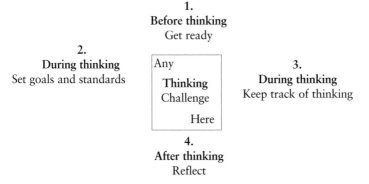

	1. **Before thinking** Get ready	
2. **During thinking** Set goals and standards	Any Thinking Challenge Here	**3.** **During thinking** Keep track of thinking
	4. **After thinking** Reflect	

Figure 6.01: FourThought Strategy (Tishman, Perkins and Jay 1995: p.78)

This is proposed as a means to assist pupils to become good *mental managers*, that is, to develop the metacognitive skills that are needed for good thinking. It is intended to assist pupils to avoid the typical pitfalls in thinking that can occur at each of three thinking junctures, 'before', 'during' and 'after' a thinking challenge:

> The **'before thinking' pitfall** occurs when people plunge into a thinking challenge without adequate mental preparation – without taking the time to clear their minds, to focus their thoughts, and to visualize what's upcoming. This pitfall can cause hasty and unfocused thinking. ...
>
> The **'during thinking' pitfall** occurs when people proceed through a thinking challenge without taking account of the larger picture – without taking the time to set goals and standards, and without making the effort to stand back and monitor how their thinking is going. This pitfall leads to an array of problems, including narrow thinking, one-dimensional thinking, and unimaginative thinking.
>
> The **'after thinking' pitfall** occurs when, at the close of a thinking challenge, people neglect to take time to reflect on how thinking went. Partially, this occurs because of a lack of opportunity. In the ever faster-paced school curriculum, the rush for coverage overtakes us, and we are rarely able to provide the time for students to conscientiously reflect on work they have just completed. But even if time for reflection is available, the habit of reflection is by and large a learned habit ... We're almost always in a hurry, and in humankind's rush to get on with life, the reflective temperament must be cultivated.
>
> (Tishman *et al.* 1995: pp.68–9)

All four steps of *FourThought* do not need to be used together. Each can be thought of as a mini-strategy that can be put to work on its own. Suggestions for each step are:

Step 1: Before thinking – get ready
• take a moment of quiet time
• visualise the upcoming topic of thought.

Step 2: During thinking – set goals and standards
• set goals
• use standards.

Step 3: During thinking – keep track of thinking
• periodically, monitor how well you are meeting your goals
• remember to play the role of mental manager.

Step 4: After thinking – reflect
- review and evaluate thinking
- look for improvements.

(Tishman et al. 1995: pp.78–82)

The idea is that these thinking moves should permeate classroom activities and become part of the classroom culture. This is a short vignette of a practical music lesson which involves all four steps:

Step 1: Before thinking – get ready
Teacher: 'Take the next minute to quietly focus your mind on your performance. Take a few deep breaths ... Clear your mind of any clutter.'

Step 2: During thinking – set goals and standards
Teacher: 'What are our goals for this performance?'
Pupil: 'To practise for the Christmas show.'
Teacher: 'And ...?'
Another pupil: 'To make the tune sound like real music, like in the film.'
Teacher: 'What does your playing need to be like for your performance to sound musical?'
Another pupil: 'We have to listen to each other so that we play the notes together.'
Teacher: 'What else?' ...

Step 3: During thinking – keep track of thinking
Teacher: 'You've played the tune through once. Are you keeping track of how well you are playing?'

Step 4: After thinking – reflect
The teacher poses a number of questions: 'Was it a good performance?' 'What was hard to do?' 'What was easy to do?' 'What could you do next time to perform even better?'

Thinking point 1

1   Do you agree with Tishman, Perkins and Jay's analysis of common thinking pitfalls? (Do you recognise them in your own thinking or your pupils' thinking? Can you give any concrete examples?)

2   Are the steps they recommend ones that you use habitually when teaching? If not, inject these thinking moves into lessons and find out if they are helpful.

3   How important a role does metacognition play in developing thinking?

A lesson framework for infusing the teaching of critical and creative thinking into content instruction

Robert Swartz and his colleagues at the National Center for Teaching Thinking (NCTT) in Massachusetts have produced lesson design handbooks to assist teachers to infuse the teaching of critical and creative thinking into content instruction – www.nctt.net. There is one for elementary grades in US schools (primary), one for secondary science, and three for language arts designed for different elementary stages. The approach is now being used across the world – in the middle East and far East, Australia and New Zealand, parts of South America, Canada and the UK.

In the handbook for elementary grades, Swartz and Parks (1994) explain infusion as blending explicit instruction in thinking skills and thinking processes with content instruction, using methods which enhance pupils' thinking and their comprehension of the content.

Types of skilful thinking

As is discussed in Chapter 2, the types of skilful thinking that they identify fall into three main categories of skills:

- generating ideas (creative thinking skills)
- clarifying ideas (which involve analysis and enhance our understanding and ability to use information) and
- assessing the reasonableness of ideas (critical thinking skills which lead to good judgement).

Decision-making and problem-solving are described as 'thinking processes' rather than individual 'thinking skills' because they each demand the integrated use of a range of thinking skills. Swartz and Parks argue that teaching the thinking skills involved in generating ideas, clarifying ideas and assessing the reasonableness of ideas, without helping pupils learn how to combine them for successful decision-making and problem-solving, accomplishes only part of the task of teaching thinking. Also, if one teaches strategies for problem-solving and decision-making, without teaching pupils the thinking skills needed to use these strategies effectively, this is similarly limited (Swartz and Parks 1994: p.8).

Swartz and Parks claim that often the problem-solving examples found in mathematics and science texts provide an inadequate context to teach skilful problem-solving, since they are intended to give pupils practice in applying mathematical or scientific principles rather than grappling with problems that require definition, the selection of the best solution, and implementation. The range of thinking skills that pupils use in this context is therefore quite restricted. If one relates this to Lauren Resnick's working definition of higher order thinking, one can see immediately that typical mathematics and science problems from textbooks lack some of the features implied by this definition.

Teaching methods

A range of teaching methods is used in infusion lessons for different purposes:

- to teach the thinking skills and processes
- to foster thinking collaboratively
- to prompt pupils to learn content thoughtfully, and
- to promote thoughtful habits of mind.

Direct instruction is used to promote clarity and reflection about the thinking skill or process.

Guided practice is woven through the lesson with pupils carrying out their thinking in a social context. *Individual thinking is blended with group interaction* to show pupils how the interplay of ideas can enhance their thinking.

Thoughtful learning of the content is prompted through a *variety of methods* appropriate to the content and pupils' level of cognitive development, such as asking higher order questions, inviting pupils' questions, 'hands-on' investigation and essay writing.

Thoughtful habits of mind are promoted through the *teacher modelling his or her own thinking dispositions*, for example, by asking clarifying questions, allowing time for pupils to respond thoughtfully to questions, using precision in language and promoting precision of expression.

The four components of the lesson

An infusion lesson has four distinct components: introduction, thinking actively, thinking about thinking, and applying the thinking.

In the *introduction* component, a discussion or activity:

- demonstrates to pupils what they already know about the thinking skill or process being taught; or not?
- shows pupils why this type of thinking is important and relates its importance to their own experience; and
- introduces them to the process of engaging in the thinking skilfully and the significance of doing this in relation to the content they are learning.

In the *thinking actively* component, verbal prompts (usually questions) and graphic organisers (to reinforce the verbal prompts) are used to guide pupils through the thinking activity. A 'thinking map' is provided for each thinking skill and process and pupils may instead produce their own. For example, the 'thinking map' and graphic organiser for skilful decision-making look like this (see Figures 6.02 and 6.03):

SKILFUL DECISION-MAKING

1 What makes a decision necessary?
2 What are my options?
3 What information is there about the consequences of each option?
4 How important are the consequences?
5 Which option is best in light of the consequences?

Figure 6.02: A Thinking Map for Skilful Decision-Making (Swartz and Parks, National Center for Teaching Thinking)

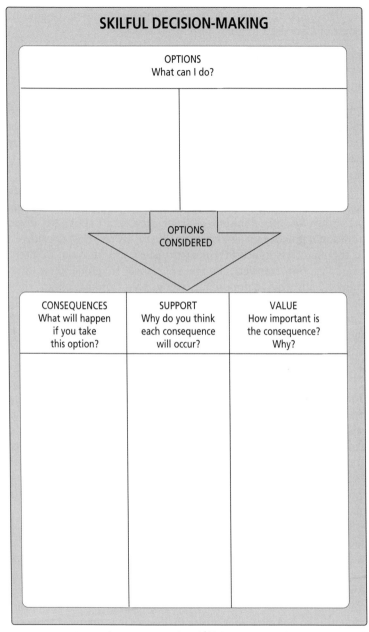

Figure 6.03: A Graphic Organiser for Skilful Decison-Making (Swartz and Parks, National Center for Teaching Thinking)

In the *thinking about thinking* component, three organising questions are used to guide pupils' reflections:

- What kinds of thinking did you engage in?
- How did you carry out this kind of thinking?
- Is this an effective way to engage in this kind of thinking?

Pupils then develop their own explicit written plan to guide their thinking when a similar need arises in future. This component of the lesson therefore serves both a retrospective function by bringing to pupils' consciousness the structure of the thinking they just did, and a prospective function.

Finally, in the *applying the thinking* component teachers are reminded to use different types of examples to demonstrate the versatility of the thinking skill or process. Pupils are given additional practice on similar examples to the one they considered in the main lesson activity (near transfer) and on quite different examples (far transfer). Pupils are asked to guide their own thinking in this component, using the thinking plan they developed in the *thinking about thinking* component of the lesson. There should be reinforcement of the same thinking throughout the school year.

Contexts for lessons and assessment

To encourage teachers to create their own infusion lessons there is a lesson plan template, and, for each thinking skill and process, a completed lesson plan and list of examples, suggested by teachers, of lesson contexts classified by grade level (for US schools), subject and topic. There is a set of exemplar lessons at www.nctt.net/lessonsarticles.html#LESSONS. These focus on the following thinking skills – compare and contrast (three lessons); decision-making (three lessons); and problem-solving (one lesson) – and the following areas of the curriculum: language, science, social subjects and mathematics.

Teachers are advised to take great care when choosing contexts for infusion lessons. The key is to find a context that offers rich development of the thinking process and rich instruction of the content objective. There are two extremes to be avoided: the content is so complex that it overshadows the thinking activity to the extent that the pupil remembers the content but not the thinking process; or the content is not well developed (it is superficially touched upon to provide a vehicle for teaching thinking) so that the pupil learns little about the subject. This difficulty was brought out in Chapter 4.

The last section in the lesson plan template is on assessment of the thinking skill or process. The advice here is that teachers can use the transfer and reinforcement examples to assess the thinking skill or ability, taking note of pupils' responses or actions. For example, in order to assess problem-solving, you can ask pupils to think through a solution to a problem:

> Make sure the problems you suggest to students are authentic and open-ended and need defining in order to get the most comprehensive profile of your students' problem-solving abilities. Ask students to use a graphic organizer to record their ideas, but let them choose which one they will work with. Also ask them to write down their plan for implementing their solution. Make sure they are raising the questions on the thinking map as they try to solve the problems ...
>
> (Swartz and Parks 1994: p.86)

Alternatively, give a problem-solving task to do:

> ask them to plan out their performances. This should provide some information about their problem-solving abilities. As you observe their performance, note how they identify problems, think through possible solutions, and make judgments about the best solution. If you have trouble ascertaining whether they are doing this, you can interview the students after they have completed the task.
>
> (Swartz and Parks 1994: p.86)

For an example of a decision-making lesson – Mr Arable and the Runt Pig – see the NCTT website. It is a language lesson for middle primary stages and it gives a detailed account of each component, extracted from the handbook for elementary grades.

Thinking point 2

1   Visit the NCTT website to view the exemplar lessons and articles. Look for potential applications of this approach in your current teaching plan. Implement an infusion lesson in an age-appropriate way.

2   Evaluate the lesson.

The Activating Children's Thinking Skills (ACTS) Project in Northern Ireland

Carol McGuinness and her colleagues at Queen's University, Belfast have worked with teachers of Key Stage 2 pupils in Northern Ireland primary schools to develop and research into infusion lessons which are based on the ideas of Swartz and Parks. The ACTS project has entered a second phase, on *Sustainable Thinking Classrooms* (referred to as ACTS II). A lesson handbook has been produced with this title (McGuinness, Sheehy, Curry and Eakin 2003). From extensive experience, the team is able to offer very useful advice to teachers who are working to implement the approach in their schools. For example, a list of the advantages of graphic organisers (which they refer to as thinking diagrams) has been produced:

> **Advantages of Thinking Diagrams**
> At first sight thinking diagrams may seem rather laborious as a teaching strategy but they do have certain advantages:
> - They help to make the steps in thinking more explicit for both pupils and teachers;
> - They slow down the thinking process so that pupils have time to grasp what might be involved;
> - They keep an external record of earlier steps in the thinking process so that pupils and teachers can more easily look back and reflect on earlier stages and on the whole process;
> - They can be used for work with individual pupils, groups and whole class teaching;
> - Thinking diagrams can be simplified or made more complex depending on the age and level of the pupils;
> - Teachers can construct their own diagrams to suit different thinking activities;
> - They can be used as classroom posters to illustrate 'models of thinking';
> - They can be used as prompts for subsequent written work by pupils and as the basis for assessing written work.

Another very important aspect which is focused on, and which many Scottish teachers raise on my courses, is the *quality of groupwork* in their classrooms. Because some teachers feel that pupils don't appear to work very productively when placed in groups (some groups go 'off task', not everyone in the group contributes equally to the work, there are disagreements among the group members etc.), they are resistant to any approaches to developing pupils' thinking which involve collaborative learning or group discussion. Other teachers may be used to a more traditional approach in which the teacher introduces the lesson and the pupils are then given individual work to do. This is how this issue is discussed in the handbook:

Classroom Talk in Thinking Classrooms

By now you will recognise that enhancing thinking and developing pupils' capacity for more effective thinking and learning depends to a large extent on the type and the quality of both teacher–pupil and pupil–pupil talk in classrooms. Increasingly it is recognised that knowledge and alternative strategies for thinking are socially constructed in the classroom through dialogue and discussion among pupils and between pupils and teachers. To get the most benefit from such dialogue, classrooms need to be organized and managed in certain ways.

Facilitating classroom talk with groups

Most approaches to teaching thinking recommend that pupils engage in collaborative work either in small groups or in pairs. Teachers differ in how they organise their classrooms and particularly in the amount of groupwork they use. Before launching the ACTS teaching strategies, teachers have found it helpful to reconsider the quality of groupwork in their classrooms and:

- To engage in prior discussion with the pupils about the purposes of working together.
- To set (or get the class to set) ground rules for working in groups; for example, only one person can speak at a time, everybody listens, giving others a chance to speak (turn-taking), encouraging quiet ones, staying on task, doing your fair share of the work.
- To give pupils practice at working in groups.
- To assign roles in groups – chair/leader, scribe, reporter, encourager and so on (depends on the age and how experienced the pupils are in managing group tasks).
- To keep group sizes relatively small, probably 3/4 pupils, especially if the children are engaged in a genuinely co-operative task.

Finally, they offer a few gentle cautions ...

- Don't attempt too much too soon – take it in small steps.
- Teaching thinking skills is not a cure for all ills – have modest expectations, especially at the beginning.

- Don't give in to early disappointments – if your first efforts are not great, modify and push on.
- Take the longer-term view.
- Thinking, important as it is, is not the only thing pupils must learn at school!!!

Thinking point 3

1   How good is the quality of groupwork in your classes? Do you agree with some of the suggestions for improving groupwork?

2   Which other important factors would impinge on the success of infusion lessons using the Swartz and Parks approach?

KEY MESSAGES

1 Infusion lessons should have a clear and logical structure. Having distinct stages or components to the lesson enables the teacher and pupils to focus in better on the types of thinking that are needed at each stage.

2 Three thinking junctures are before, during and after a thinking challenge. Before thinking, pupils focus on the upcoming task. During thinking, pupils set goals and targets and keep track of thinking. After thinking, pupils reflect on the thinking they have just done.

3 The Swartz and Parks lesson framework includes a fourth component in which pupils apply the thinking beyond the lesson. This provides reinforcement and enables pupils to transfer the thinking skill or process in question. Assessment of thinking skills can be linked to this component.

4 Graphic organisers or thinking diagrams help make thinking steps more explicit and slow down the thinking process to enable pupils to grasp what might be involved.

5 Most approaches to teaching thinking recommend that pupils engage in collaborative work either in small groups or pairs. Teachers have found it helpful to re-examine the quality of groupwork in their classrooms.

Recommended further reading

McGuinness, C., Sheey, N., Curry, C. and Eakin, A. (2003) *ACTS II Sustainable Thinking Classrooms: A Handbook for Teachers of Key Stage 2 Pupils* Belfast: Queen's University Belfast.

A clear introduction to the principles and core concepts combined with sample lessons, thinking diagrams, practical advice on implementation, and a list of references and resources.

Swartz, R. J. and Parks, S. (1994). *Infusing the Teaching of Critical and Creative Thinking into Content Instruction* Pacific Grove: Critical Thinking Press & Software.

A very comprehensive and practical resource for any teacher or school contemplating using infusion to teach thinking. Ideas on lessons may need some modification to suit the Scottish curriculum.

Tishman, S., Perkins, D., and Jay, E. (1995) *The Thinking Classroom: Learning and Teaching in a Culture of Thinking* Needham Heights, MA: Allyn and Bacon. See chapters 6–7.

Chapters 6–7 explore the topic of mental management and introduce the FourThought Strategy.

7 Bringing it all together – cross-cutting themes

Theories on constructivist learning, metacognition, and the affective and social dimensions of thinking have a very strong bearing on the development of pupils' thinking and their ability to transfer thinking skills. The chapter begins by examining some origins of constructivist learning principles and how these may be applied in the classroom. It moves on to explore the concept of metacognition with reference to John Flavell's analysis and John Nisbet and Janet Shucksmith's research in Scottish primary classrooms in the 1980s. The metacognitive component within a range of current approaches to teaching thinking is analysed with reference to discussions in previous chapters. Finally, the influences of emotions, feelings and social interaction on the development of pupils' thinking are examined, with a particular emphasis on motivation to learn.

Constructivist learning and developing thinking

In Chapter 5, the following definition of a thinking task was presented:

> A thinking task is essentially one which asks pupils to use their existing knowledge in order to generate new knowledge – to come up with a good example, generate a set of options when a decision has to be taken, predict the outcome of an experiment and later compare this with the actual outcome, make a good plan, evaluate their solution, and so on.

Learning, according to constructivist perspectives, requires learners to use what they already know to grapple with new information and scenarios. Subject knowledge is therefore extended from something to be mastered to becoming the stimulus to reasoning (Leat and Higgins 2002).

Some of the origins of constructivist theories can be traced back to John Dewey (1859–1952) who was one of America's most important philosophers and learning theorists. The key to genuine learning, according to Dewey, was purposeful activity in social settings. He wanted schools to engage pupils in meaningful activities which involved collaborative working on problems. The teacher's task was to:

> 'provide the conditions that stimulate thinking' and to take a sympathetic attitude; the teacher had to participate in 'a common or conjoint experience' with the learner. Under no circumstances was just telling the student about a new idea very effective–the student would come to learn this new thing by rote, but would be unlikely to understand it or see its relevance and connection to other ideas.
>
> (Phillips and Soltis 2004: p.56)

According to Dewey, meaningful problems must emerge from situations that fall within pupils' interests and experiences. He did not mean by this that pupils should not be extended or that their intellectual horizons should not be stretched, rather it was a matter of where the teacher started and how learning proceeded (2004: p.39).

According to the Swiss psychologist Jean Piaget (1896–1980), when children encounter a new experience they both 'accommodate' their existing thinking to it and 'assimilate' aspects of it. In so doing they move beyond one state of mental 'equilibration' and restructure their thoughts to create another. Through this process children gradually come to construct more detailed, complex and accurate understandings of the phenomena they experience. Piaget identified characteristic stages in the successive development of mental structures, as follows:

- the sensori-motor stage (approximately birth–two years)
- the pre-operational stage (approximately 2–7 years)
- the concrete operations stage (approximately 7–12 years)
- the formal operations stage (approximately 12 years upwards)

It is only at the stage of formal operations that abstract thinking is believed to be possible (Pollard 2002: pp.138–9).

Like Dewey, the Russian psychologist Lev Vygotsky (1896–1934) was also very aware of the social nature of learning. He did not assign much importance to the child's 'stage' of development (in the Piagetian sense), viewing this as a rather static indicator of what intellectual tasks a child could accomplish on his or her own. He was more interested in the learning potential that the child might have, that is, what he or she might accomplish with adult guidance or in collaboration with more capable peers (Vygotsky 1978). Vygotsky recognised that a key factor in social learning was learning by imitation: 'Interacting with adults and peers in co-operative social settings gave the young learner ample opportunity to observe, imitate, and subsequently develop higher mental functioning.' (Phillips and Soltis, 2004: p.59)

A contemporary movement in education known as *Constructivism* has since emerged. This complex movement, according to Phillips and Soltis (2004: p.50), consists of a number of 'sometimes warring and quite incompatible' sects. Perkins (1999) uses the expression 'vexed and messy landscape' to describe it. This book is not the place to examine the competing positions that are taken by experts on constructivist learning. The important questions for teachers who are interested in teaching along constructivist lines are, can any key principles be discerned, and how can they be translated into practice?

Pollard (2002) contrasts three key learning perspectives, Behaviourism, Constructivism and Social constructivism, in terms of learner image, images of teaching and learning, characteristic child activities (and two other elements) as follows:

	Behaviourism in classrooms	Constructivism in classrooms	Social constructivism in classrooms
Image of learner	• Passive • Individual • Extrinsically motivated	• Active • Individual • Intrinsically motivated	• Active • Social • Socially motivated
Images of teaching and learning	• Teacher transmits knowledge and skills • Learning depends on teaching and systematic reinforcement of correct behaviours	• Teacher gives child opportunity to construct knowledge and skills gradually through experience • Learning can be independent of teaching	• Knowledge and skills constructed gradually through experience, interaction and adult support • Learning comes through the interdependence of teacher and children
Characteristic child activities	• Class listening to an adult • Class working on an exercise	• Individuals making, experimenting, playing or otherwise doing something	• Class, group or individual discussion with an adult or other child/ren • Group problem-solving

(Pollard 2002: p.145)

Phillips and Soltis argue that a good constructivist teacher will be indistinguishable from a good progressive educator who works according to Dewey's principles:

> Students will be actively engaged with interesting and relevant problems; they will be able to discuss with each other and with the teacher; they will be active inquirers rather than passive; they will have adequate time to reflect: they will have opportunities to test or evaluate the knowledge that they have constructed; and they will reflect seriously about the constructions produced by other students and by the teacher.
>
> (2004: p.52)

In the above quotation, Phillips and Soltis reflect a social constructivism perspective, but this does not preclude individual reflection and inquiry. Opportunities for quiet reflection and individual work should form part of the experience that pupils have at school.

Perkins (1999, pp.6–7) identifies three distinct roles in constructivism, the *active learner*, the *social learner* and the *creative learner*:

Knowledge and understanding as actively acquired. Instead of just reading, listening and working through routine exercises, learners discuss, debate, hypothesize, investigate, and take viewpoints.

Knowledge and understanding as socially constructed. Learners do not construct knowledge and understanding individually, instead knowledge and understanding are co-constructed in dialogue with others. The teaching of history should make learners aware of how historical 'truth' varies with the interest groups. The teaching of science should lead learners to recognize that scientific truths are arrived at by a social process of critical scrutiny.

Knowledge and understanding as created or recreated. Often constructivists hold that learners need to create or recreate knowledge for themselves. It is not enough that they assume an active stance. Teachers should guide them to rediscover historical perspectives, scientific truths, and so on.

Perkins observes that these three perspectives are not always combined in practice:

> Teachers can organise learning experiences in active ways that do not require learners to engage in testing and building knowledge in a social manner or to invent or reinvent theories or viewpoints.
>
> (Perkins 1999: p.7)

Brooks and Brooks (2001: pp.150–7) assert that becoming a constructivist teacher is not as overwhelming as many teachers think. They identify ten constructivist teaching behaviours which are intended to provide a usable framework within which teachers can experiment. Constructivist teachers ...

1 encourage and accept student autonomy and initiative;
2 use raw data and primary sources, along with manipulative, interactive and physical materials;
3 use cognitive terminology such as 'classify', 'analyse', 'predict' and 'create', when framing tasks;
4 allow student responses to drive lessons, shift instructional strategies, and alter content;
5 inquire about students' understandings of concepts before sharing their own understandings of those concepts;
6 encourage students to engage in dialogue, both with the teacher and with one another;
7 encourage student inquiry by asking thoughtful, open-ended questions and encouraging students to ask questions of each other;
8 seek elaboration of students' initial responses;
9 engage students in experiences that might engender contradictions to students' initial hypotheses and then encourage discussion; and
10 allow wait time after posing questions.

Each of these teacher behaviours is elaborated, for example, in relation to 10, 'allow wait time after posing questions', some key points are:

• In classroom environments that require immediate responses, some students are forced to be spectators as their quicker peers react.
• Such environments prevent students from thinking through issues and concepts thoroughly.

- The rapid fire approach does not provide an opportunity for the teacher to sense the manner in which most of the students have understood the questions.
- In addition to increasing wait time, students working in small groups can be encouraged to consider the answers to questions before the whole group is invited back together to report on their deliberations.

The first teacher behaviour, 'encourage and accept student autonomy and initiative', requires that the classroom should be run along democratic lines, thus contributing towards education for citizenship. The combination of these teaching behaviours should result in a classroom which functions as a genuine learning community.

Thus we begin to build up a picture of what a constructivist classroom might look like. But it is clear that anyone walking into a school where all of the teachers teach along constructivist lines would discover a diversity of learning and teaching practices! Perkins (1999) argues that constructivist techniques must be deployed wisely, in the right place for the right purpose. They should be targeted as a response to the learners' difficulties. While there are strong reasons for adopting constructivist approaches, such as the observation (borne out by research evidence) that with traditional methods there are persistent shortfalls in pupils' understanding and a great deal of passive knowledge, nevertheless some complications can arise:

Constructivist techniques often require more time than do traditional educational practices – a cost worth paying, enthusiasts say, but many teachers feel the pressures and conclude that they need to make compromises. Asking learners to discover or rediscover principles can foster understanding, but learners sometimes persist in discovering the wrong principles – for example, an idiosyncratic scientific theory. Although ardent constructivists may argue that process is all, others believe that one way or another, students need to arrive at an understanding of the best theories propounded by the disciplines.

(Perkins 1999: p.7)

Brooks and Brooks (2001: p.150) identify three common reasons for teachers resisting constructivist approaches. The first is commitment to their present instructional approach, the second is concern about pupil learning and the third is a concern about classroom control. They comment that in today's climate, the key to pupil and school success is higher test scores, and that it is difficult for teachers to embrace teaching practices designed to enable pupils to construct meaning in such a regressive climate. My personal response to this present difficulty, which affects us too in Scotland, is that the time is long overdue for the profession and other stakeholders to weigh up the real educational costs of neglecting to teach for understanding. Furthermore, we might consider how teaching along constructivist lines could better equip children to transfer their learning to new situations. Constructivist learners, through actively seeking connections with their existing knowledge and experiences whenever any new learning situations are encountered, integrate new knowledge more effectively and meaningfully than those who attempt to learn by rote. They are more likely to bring their existing knowledge and skills successfully to bear whenever new learning situations are encountered.

Thinking point 1
Where do you position yourself in relation to constructivist learning theories and constructivist teaching approaches?

The role of metacognition in developing thinking and fostering transfer

John Flavell at Stanford University is credited with introducing the term 'metacognition' in 1970 to describe the monitoring of one's thinking. He defines and explains the concept as follows:

> 'Metacognition' refers to one's knowledge concerning one's own cognitive processes ... For example, I am engaged in metacognition ... if I notice that I am having more trouble learning A than B; if it strikes me that I should double-check C before accepting it as a fact; if it occurs to me that I had better scrutinize each and every alternative in any multiple-choice type task situation before deciding which is the best one; if I sense that I had better make a note of D because I may forget it ... Metacognition refers ... to the active monitoring and consequent regulation and orchestration of these processes ... usually in the service of some concrete goal or objective.
>
> (Flavell 1976: p.232)

Flavell suggests that *metacognitive experiences* – such as 'I notice that I am having more trouble learning A than B' – act as a kind of quality control on thinking. *Metacognitive strategies* – such as '... I should double-check C ...' – provide a means to regulate one's thinking.

John Nisbet and Janet Shucksmith (1986) have developed some of these ideas by conducting research on learning strategies in Scottish primary classrooms. They believe that:

> Learning to learn must be done in a real context: the best way to acquire strategies of learning is in the process of learning. But if what is learned is to be transferable to other contexts, then it must be taught in such a way as to encourage transfer.
>
> (Nisbet and Shucksmith 1986: p.94)

They distinguish between skills and strategies by defining strategies as being a level above skills. Many skills are taught and learned in the context of specific subjects or situations, such as using a lathe. Some general skills are specific to tasks shared in related subjects, such as using a dictionary or plotting points on a graph. A strategy involves putting skills together with a conscious purpose, not just on instruction or demand. A strategy is more modifiable and flexible in nature than a skill, which is more 'reflexive'. In order to apply a strategy you must possess a range of skills, be aware of a range of possible strategies, and select appropriately from these. This implies the capacity to transfer skills and strategies to fit new situations (Nisbet and Shucksmith 1984).

They observed that strategies tend to be taught in specific contexts – planning for projects, checking for arithmetic, self-testing for spelling, and so on – and children are rarely taught to generalise them. Of four criteria that they identify for skills training – mastery, retention, durability and transfer – only the first three seem to receive much attention. When they set out to find examples of classrooms where children were being set significant challenges which would develop their use of strategic thinking, they were disappointed:

> there were many time-filling tasks and much 'busy work' which did not demand mental effort. There was reinforcement and over-learning, but we did not often find the teaching or encouragement of strategies which we were looking for.
>
> (Nisbet and Shucksmith 1984: pp.12–13)

Of course, these observations were made almost quarter of a century ago; perhaps they don't apply to present-day classrooms. Nisbet and Shucksmith recommend that for learning strategies to transfer, they must first be consciously articulated and then practised so that eventually they become part of an habitual unconscious approach to learning. Conscious articulation involves identifying the variety of sub-skills which are then built into sequences or strategies for tackling problems. Practice is necessary, since otherwise by constantly having to think about what you are doing you may inhibit your capacity to do it.

The methods that Nisbet and Shucksmith propose for improving children's capacity to think and work strategically comprise direct instruction of strategies, modelling of strategies and encouraging metacognitive skills. Pupils should also be allowed to explore their own metacognitive knowledge by discussion and exposure to a variety of contexts or circumstances where it is called into play. These methods were discussed in Chapter 6.

How does all this apply to the discussion and practical examples of thinking tasks presented in earlier chapters, and what can be learned about approaches to developing metacognition when these are taken together? I shall examine the references to metacognition in the order in which they were encountered within earlier chapters.

The importance of pupils developing a *strategic approach to learning* was raised in Chapter 1. This enables pupils to become autonomous learners, for example, they are able to set personal learning goals, make plans, and evaluate their own performances.

Chapter 2 presented Resnick's working definition of higher order thinking, in which metacognition emerges as a key element:

> Higher order thinking involves self-regulation of the thinking process. We do not recognise higher order thinking in an individual when someone else 'calls the plays' at every step.
>
> (Resnick 1987: p.3)

When Perkins examines the influence of the social context on the development of thinking dispositions, he notes:

> The discourse also produces more metacognition – more explicit recognition of the thinking moves in play – simply because the participants need to articulate their thoughts to communicate and

thus make their patterns of thinking more salient and subject to examination.

(Perkins 2001: p.159)

Thus, through participating in the discussion, the learner has become more self-consciously aware of his or her own thinking processes (one would describe this as *metacognitive awareness*).

In Chapter 3, I explained how pupils who were learning to solve programming problems were encouraged to:

Step 1: reflect back on their own processes of problem solving.
Step 2: abstract some general principles of effective problem solving.
Step 3: articulate these principles in their own words.
Step 4: explore other contexts where these principles could be applied.

Engagement in these four processes – reflection, abstraction, articulation, exploration – is intended, in combination, to provide a powerful stimulus for *metacognitive reflection*, to develop pupils' *strategic thinking*, and to lay the foundations for pupils to be able to *transfer* the skills and strategies more widely. Engaging learners in these four processes should help them to make richer connections between previous learning experiences and new learning experiences.

When recounting elements of *Instrumental Enrichment*, an illustration of the dynamic interaction that takes place between the teacher and pupil *during mediation* was presented:

witness a student deeply engaged in a cognitive task of searching for a pattern that connects the seemingly random series of dots and listen closely to the expert intervention of the teacher-coach: 'Why did you do that?' 'What were you thinking just now?' 'How does this remind you of another problem we did, yesterday?'

(Fogarty 2001: p.146)

In this example, the teacher has gone beyond the cognitive and into the realm of the *metacognitive* by prompting pupils, as the activity unfolds, to think about their thinking through a process of guided reflection. It contains an instance of the teacher encouraging backward-reaching transfer: 'How does this remind you of another problem we did, yesterday?' (Perkins and Salomon 2001: p.373)

The CASE network website explains how a CASE lesson is different from 'discovery' learning:

> This is not 'discovery' learning where the teacher tries to elicit the 'correct' explanation. The teacher's role in metacognition is to help students to articulate the type of thinking that has been used to solve a particular problem and to identify 'why' a particular strategy was used and 'how' such a strategy could be utilised in the future.

Here the emphasis is upon engaging pupils in metacognitive reflection *after* the activity in order to enhance pupils' strategic knowledge and the prospect of them being able to transfer the strategies to new problem-solving contexts in a forward-reaching direction.

In Chapter 5, I recounted how Leat and Higgins (2002) identify one of the key characteristics of powerful pedagogical strategies, such as *Odd One Out,* as their use to provide a springboard to reflect upon in a class debriefing discussion, which helps with developing metacognitive awareness.

Fisher's set of general questions which can be posed before, during and after each thinking game are designed to engage strategic thinking and metacognition:

> [before] What other games do you know that are like this game? Can you give examples?
> [during] What do you need to do to win, or achieve your target in the game?
> [after] What strategy did you use in playing the game? Was it a good strategy?
>
> (Fisher 1997: pp.7–8)

Schoenfeld's method of actively intervening through questioning as pupils work on problems is designed to encourage them to *monitor* and *regulate* their own thinking processes:

> *What (exactly) are you doing?*
> (Can you describe it to me precisely?)
> *Why are you doing it?*
> (How does it fit into the solution?)
> *How does it help you?*
> (What will you do with the outcome when you obtain it?)
>
> (Schoenfeld 1989: p.98)

Tishman, Perkins and Jay's (1995) four building blocks for strategic thinking – *state, search, evaluate* and *elaborate* – when taught using a combination of direct instruction, teacher modelling and engaging pupils in metacognition, should enable pupils to construct their *own* strategies for solving problems.

The *FourThought* Strategy (Tishman, Perkins and Jay 1995) discussed in Chapter 6 is intended to assist pupils to become good *mental managers*, that is, to develop the metacognitive skills that are needed for good thinking. It is intended to assist pupils to avoid the typical pitfalls in thinking that can occur at each of three thinking junctures, 'before', 'during' and 'after' a thinking challenge. Thus it has an entirely metacognitive focus.

The developers suggest that all four steps of *FourThought* do not need to be used together Each can be thought of as a mini-strategy that can be put to work on its own. The idea is that these thinking moves should permeate classroom activities and become part of the classroom culture.

Finally, in the Swartz and Parks infusion lesson approach, the third lesson component: *Thinking about thinking*, ensures that teachers build in time during the lesson for metacognitive reflection.

From all these examples, three clear messages emerge:
- Metacognition is an essential element of developing good thinking and fostering transfer.
- Metacognition should permeate classroom activities, before, during and after a thinking challenge.
- The pacing of lessons needs to be adjusted to make room for metacognition to develop.

Thinking point 2

1 Do you agree with Nisbet and Shucksmith when they say that learning to learn must be done in a real context?

2 Have present-day classrooms changed markedly from the situation that Nisbet and Shucksmith found during their research?

3 How can the pacing of lessons be adjusted to make room for metacognition to develop? Can there be too much metacognition going on in classrooms? What are the consequences if metacognition is insufficiently focused upon?

The affective and social dimensions of thinking

Nisbet highlights the central role of emotions and feelings in thinking:

> We need to build on the satisfactions of thinking, not be preoccupied with the difficulties or the shame of failure. Resolving a difficulty, understanding a complex topic, the flash of insight in solving a problem: these are (or should be) deeply satisfying experiences. Confusion and inability to comprehend are frustrating and quickly erode the will to learn or to try.
>
> (Nisbet 1990 p.4)

This is a view that most people can relate to extremely well, no matter how successful they may consider themselves to be as learners. It is a salutary experience to reflect on just how often our pupils enjoy the satisfactions of thinking during lessons. For some young people the willingness to learn or to try may already have been eroded. The real challenge facing the teacher is to find creative ways to tip the scales towards the 'satisfactions of thinking' and away from 'confusion and inability to comprehend'.

In curriculum documents and official advice, teachers are frequently exhorted to set challenging problems for their pupils to do. If problems are 'well pitched' in terms of their difficulty – not too easy but not too difficult either – this enhances the prospect of pupils being able to experience a sense of satisfaction, since they are able to make some progress with the problem, and hopefully, come up with their own solutions in the end. It is worthwhile, at this point, to return to Polya's (1948) advice on giving help and asking questions (see Chapter 4, Thinking point 2):

> The teacher should help, not too much and not too little, to give the student a reasonable share of the work. If the student is unable to do much the teacher should leave him some illusion of independent work. It is best to help the student naturally – by asking a question or indicating a step that could have occurred to the student himself – and also unobtrusively – by stating the question or suggestion generally to leave plenty for the student to do.

If one follows Polya's advice, it should not be assumed, when choosing a suitable problem, that the level of difficulty need be such that the pupil should be able to solve the problem completely unaided. In accordance with Vygotsky's social perspective on learning, it may be much more beneficial to select problems which pupils might accomplish in collaboration with more (or other) capable peers and with teacher guidance. When teachers select problems which pupils can do without their assistance this is often for classroom management reasons, rather than primarily educational reasons, although it should go without saying that an unruly classroom is not a place where any young person can learn effectively.

The social constructivist perspective does not place the teacher as the only learning resource in the classroom; peer learning is a very important ingredient. If the teacher plans activities which involve peer learning, it is possible to set more challenging problems for pupils to do. Peer learning does not imply that all activities should be group tasks. What it does imply is that, whether pupils are working on group activities or individual tasks, they should be encouraged, and supported by the teacher through demonstration, advice and guidance, to support each others' learning. This can happen for pupils of all ages, even very young pupils who are learning the social skills of good communication and co-operating together.

Every pupil should have opportunities to discuss their work, ask questions, explain their ideas or solutions, demonstrate techniques, coach other pupils and peer assess as part of the normal classroom interaction that goes on between peers, and between pupil and teacher. As a way of making some of these ideas more concrete, I shall quote from my own research notes with an S3 computing studies class in which pupils were given considerable autonomy about how they worked on programming problems:

> It was my impression from working with the class, from examination of their work, and from interviews, that there was far more collaboration actually going on between pupils such as Paula and Lorraine, Bryan and Scott, and Kathleen and Claudia, than their responses in the unit 1 questionnaire seem to indicate. For example, although Paula had indicated a preference for working on her own, I asked her if she and Lorraine, who sat beside her all through S3, worked together on problems (it turned out, to my surprise and also the class teacher's, that they were cousins!):

P: We did – I think we did that at the beginning, then we worked on our own. It was okay – I like Lorraine, she's my cousin – so it was good working with her, but I prefer to work on my own because you can go at your own speed. Sometimes she goes faster than me, then she has to wait on me – or if I go faster than her on something, then she's still trying to write something out...

MK: So did you both decide that you would just work ahead at your own pace?

P: Yes.

MK: Were you still able to help each other?

P: Yes. If there was something wrong and we didn't understand anything or did something wrong – we asked each other – spoke to each other. But one time she put a lot of her program in as comments after the flashes. She was wondering why it wasn't printing! [laughs] Then things I did – if I made a mistake, she'd point it out – 'You've done that' – and I'd go back and fix it. Things that you don't really notice on your own.

MK: Did you just tell her what was wrong, or did you help her to find out for herself?

P: I just told her!

MK: Did she appreciate you doing that?

P: Yes.

MK: Do you think that, although you just told her what was wrong, she understood what was wrong?

P: I think so [sounding hesitant].

It seems from this account – and also Lorraine's – that they had found a productive way of working together to give them some measure of independence from each other (and also a measure of independence from the teacher, since they were able to help each other). The benefits were not just that they were able to help each other out when they were stuck, but they were also able to monitor each other's performance (with the added bonus of having an occasional laugh at the other's mistakes!).

Teachers need to know their pupils well in order to select good problems, since pupils' aptitudes and interests will determine to quite a large extent pupils' individual responses to being given a particular problem to solve. A problem is not a genuine problem to the pupil, if he or she has no real interest in solving it. It becomes merely an exercise, a hoop to jump through, in order to keep the teacher happy and stay out of trouble, or something to be avoided, leading to 'off task' behaviour.

Another important issue is the pacing of lessons. If certain pupils rarely get the opportunity to finish a problem because they are slower workers than the rest of the class, and all of the class has to move on to the next lesson, then those pupils are being denied the opportunity to experience that sense of satisfaction which comes when a solution is finally worked out. If this becomes a regular event, they will soon not see the point in putting in effort, and a vicious circle will be created.

Teachers also need to be able to differentiate effectively in order to cater for a range of learning needs. It is not however possible, or desirable, to construct an individual curriculum for every child in the class. Rather the goal should be that every pupil experiences a sense of being intellectually and emotionally engaged in tasks and activities.

This discussion points to why the social setting in the classroom is important, both to support the development of thinking and to create the disposition to engage in higher order thinking. The view of *knowledge and understanding as socially constructed* (Perkins 1999) – 'Learners do not construct knowledge and understanding individually, instead knowledge and understanding are co-constructed in dialogue with others' – leads towards collaborative learning approaches.

Resnick develops the theme of thinking dispositions, which are:

> cultivated by participation in social communities that value thinking and independent judgement. Such communities communicate these values by making available many occasions for such activity and responding encouragingly to expressions of questioning and judgement. The process of learning is further aided when there are many opportunities to observe others engaging in such thinking activities.
>
> (Resnick 1987: p.42)

She outlines a range of opportunities that the social setting provides. Modelling by skilled thinkers allows pupils to become aware of mental processes that might otherwise remain implicit. 'Thinking aloud' in a social setting allows others to critique and shape one's performance. The social setting may provide a kind of scaffolding for an individual learner's initially limited performance since within the group extreme novices can participate in performing complex tasks and may eventually be able to take over most of the work. The social setting may serve to motivate pupils by encouraging them to try new, more active approaches, and through this process pupils may come to think of themselves as being capable of engaging in independent thinking and of exercising control over their own learning processes:

> Engaging in higher order thinking with others seems likely to teach students that they have the ability, the permission, and even the obligation to engage in a kind of critical analysis that does not always accept problem formulations as presented or that may challenge an accepted position.
>
> (1987: p.41)

Thus one finds in the exemplars of thinking tasks and approaches within earlier chapters a great deal of reliance on the creation of an appropriate social setting to support the development of thinking.

However, all of this has so far emphasised the positive side of thinking within social settings. Perkins (2001) cautions us to beware of some *social antagonists of thinking*, such as:

- doctrine, an official stance of a group, which no one is permitted to question;
- authoritarianism, the exercise of authority beyond its proper boundaries, which should be distinguished from legitimate authority, both political and intellectual;
- prejudice, which typically involves socially sustained and amplified stereotypes regarding other individuals and groups; and
- extreme relativism, 'Think anything you please!'.

Perkins sees all four of these as having their origins in defective thinking:

> Authority, doctrine and prejudice tell us not to notice exceptions or anomalies, and, if we do, not to think about them seriously. Relativism tells us not to worry about differences and try to puzzle out what's right.
>
> (2001: p.161)

When Lipman directs our attention to the thinking dispositions that can be fostered within a community of inquiry, such as being critical, respecting others, being inventive, seeking alternatives, co-operating intellectually, feeling a need for principles, ideals, reasons and explanations, being appreciative, consistent and self-corrective, one can see how these would serve to reduce the forces which act in opposition to good thinking.

Goleman's best-seller, *Emotional Intelligence*, has helped to raise awareness in Scottish schools of the crucial role of emotions and feelings in children's learning:

> when too many children lack the capacity to handle their upsets, to listen or focus, to rein in impulse, to feel responsible for their work or care about learning, anything that will buttress these skills will help in their education.
>
> (Goleman 1996: p.284)

Goleman suggests that emotional lessons can be built into the fabric of school life through the manner of teachers' engagements with pupils. This has resonances with Lipman's desire to see more emphasis being placed by teachers on caring thinking, which involves both thinking solicitously about the subject matter and being concerned about one's *manner* of thinking (see Chapter 2). It also has resonances with Feuerstein's *Instrumental Enrichment* programme, which was designed to overcome deficiencies in pupils' cognitive functioning including impulsive, acting-out behaviour.

From Resnick (1987), a characteristic of higher order thinking is that it is effortful. From Perkins (2001), the development of thinking dispositions too depends in part on the learner being *inclined* to use the thinking abilities that he or she possesses. Boekaerts (1988) distinguishes between 'awareness', and 'willingness' to use personal resources in the service of a learning task. She gives the following illustration:

> A good illustration of the distinction between 'awareness' and 'willingness' is that of a student who has learned via a training programme in metacognitive skills that he should double-check on coherence before he answers a comprehension question. Although this student has access to and awareness of the strategy to use, he may still fail to perform well, simply because he considers the 'extra' checking to cost too much extra time.
>
> (Boekaerts 1988: p.230)

Also she notes that exam conditions and a competitive atmosphere may elicit appraisals of the situation related to such ego-oriented goals as: 'How well can I do the task?' or 'How well can I hide my incompetence?' rather than task-oriented goals such as: 'What can

I learn from it?'. Pupils in task-oriented classes are more likely to believe that putting in effort to gain more skill will help them to succeed in life.

The theories that pupils hold about ability and intelligence can affect their willingness to expend effort. It has been found that pupils hold different conceptions of ability or 'theories of intelligence' which affect how they approach learning tasks and what they hope to gain from them (Dweck and Elliott 1983). The first theory (the 'entity' theory of intelligence) involves the belief that intelligence is a rather stable, global trait that can be judged to be adequate or inadequate. This trait is displayed in one's performance, and the judgements of that performance can indicate whether one is or is not intelligent. The second theory ('incremental') involves the belief that intellectual competence consists of a repertoire of skills that can be endlessly expanded through one's efforts. While most older children understand both views of intelligence it appears that different children, independent of their actual ability, tend to favour one or the other. As one would predict, entity theorists prefer tasks that afford opportunities to avoid mistakes and to be judged competent, whereas incremental theorists prefer tasks that afford them opportunities for learning, and they will happily immerse themselves in inquiry ('How can I do it?' 'What will I learn?').

Teachers can influence pupils towards holding an incremental view of intelligence by treating pupils' errors as natural and useful events rather than as evidence of failure, providing opportunities for pupils to engage in problem-solving and inquiry, acting as a resource and guide rather than as a judge, and applying flexible and long-term performance standards which enable progress towards targets to be recognised.

Perhaps some of these approaches could usefully be applied to *supporting positive behaviour*, where many schools nowadays seem to operate to a set of double-standards. For example, no present-day teacher would punish a child for getting a poor mark in a test, as occurred in my school days, although the teacher might suggest that more effort could go in. But some pupils get regularly excluded from school outings or other 'treats' on the grounds of their 'poor performance' at conforming to the rules for appropriate behaviour at school. Although this action is explained as a 'withdrawal of privileges', it seems to me that it is a particularly cruel form of punishment, given how much young people look forward to such events as a break from the usual school routine, and a chance to socialise with friends and perhaps get to know their teachers in a less formal setting. It is not at all in the spirit of, 'treating pupils' errors as natural and useful events', and it has the effect of excluding these pupils from the social life of the school where they would have the opportunity to form better relationships with their teachers and peers, and where they could learn to identify with being part of a caring community in which responsible behaviour is expected of everyone.

When pupils hold an incremental view of intelligence, this leads them naturally towards adopting a 'deep' approach to learning. Similarly, when teachers hold an incremental view of intelligence, this leads them naturally towards promoting a 'deep' approach to learning in their classrooms. Biggs (1988) identifies 'surface', 'deep' and 'achieving' approaches to learning as follows:

- A 'surface' approach is an approach that is embedded in pragmatism, in getting by. The student sets out to meet course requirements minimally by limiting the target to essentials that may be reproduced through rote learning. It yields outcomes which are rich in detail but poor in structure.
- A 'deep' approach is where the learner is motivated by intrinsic interest in the subject matter, and where he or she sets out to acquire competence and to discover meaning by actively seeking out connections. It yields well-structured outcomes.
- An 'achieving' approach is where the motive is ego-enhancement through achieving good grades, and the congruent strategy is organising time, working space and syllabus coverage in optimal ways. This can be combined with a surface approach (surface achieving) or a deep approach (deep achieving), for example: deep achieving is used by many of the more successful students in high school and university: they search for structure and meaning, and do so while organising their time and context optimally. (Biggs 1988: p.130)

Biggs recommends to teachers three strategies: 1) discourage a surface approach by removing those practices which induce pupils to bargain for minimal involvement – excessive assessment and workload demands, pointless busy work and pedantic course requirements, authoritarian approaches – all of which result in pressure and cynicism; 2) encourage a deep approach, through arousing pupils' interest, ensuring active involvement in learning, and encouraging reflection; and 3) develop an achieving approach, through teaching study skills in a metacognitive context.

Entwistle (1987) discusses motivation in terms of pupils' attributions of success or failure. He observes: 'Most teachers have come across pupils who, paradoxically, put effort into avoiding effort: they do all they can to avoid carrying out the tasks set by the teacher. What seems to be happening here, is that pupils are trying hard to avoid either tasks they describe as boring or situations from which they anticipate feelings of failure.' (1987: p.5–6). While fear of failure may spur on successful pupils, it may have the opposite effect on less successful pupils. External attributions of failure typically refer to bad luck, the difficulty of the task or unfairness on the teacher's part. The theory is that if pupils can be helped to move from external to internal attributions, that is, if they can be induced to take charge of their own learning, then they are more likely to increase their effort. But what if a pupil tries harder and still fails? He or she is led to a more painful attribution, that lack of ability is the cause. Entwistle argues that this conclusion is not at all inevitable, since learning strategies can be modelled and taught, and through this, pupils' learning abilities can be enhanced.

McLean (2003) views motivation for learning as coming ideally from the inside. He identifies four 'mindsets' which affect motivation:

- students' ideas about ability
- how they approach learning
- how they make sense of their progress
- how competent they feel. (2003: p.xvi)

According to McLean confidence-building schools are those which:

> instil the belief that ability is not fixed and that there are many ways to succeed. They treat mistakes as essential steps to efficacy by linking failure to factors that students can repair. Motivating schools encourage an accurate match between students' aspirations and their skills level. They praise student effort and strategy use and so help them focus on the progress of their work and make them feel responsible for success. They help students become aware of how they are smart rather than how smart they are. They emphasise the possibilities for improvement. This encourages students to put progress down to effort and concentrate on learning rather than on displaying ability. Most importantly, they stress individual, rather than normative, progress.
>
> (2003: p.xvi)

McLean argues that *the teacher's task is not to motivate students, but to provide the opportunities for achievement that will be motivating.* Teachers should help students to become self-determined through giving them chances to solve their own problems and inviting them to participate in making decisions. However McLean recognises that for some students it is difficult for teachers to find any starting point to re-engage them in learning:

> It is like looking for the start of a roll of sticky tape. All students, however, can rediscover an interest in learning, no matter how disengaged they have become. ...
>
> Disengaged students need alternative learning contexts that start from, and build on, their interests and goals. Learning needs to be connected to students' lives, involving real-life challenges and experiences, rather than imposed upon the seemingly reluctant. The starting point should be what interests and will engage different groups. Learning contexts need to provide as few obstacles and threats as possible and instead, play to students' strengths and interests and give purpose to their learning.
>
> (McLean 2003: p.129)

Thinking point 3
How important do you regard the affective and social dimensions of thinking to be? Relate this to specific situations that have occurred in your classroom.

Footnote

This chapter presents a set of powerful ideas on learning and developing thinking. To put these ideas into practice in classrooms and schools is a considerable challenge in the present climate of increasing pressure on Scottish schools to produce better and better standards. However to ignore the messages from research is to lose out on the opportunity to reconfigure the curriculum, and learning and teaching practices, in order to provide a more worthwhile education for pupils.

In my work with experienced teachers, I have become aware of how frustrated many of them feel about the circumstances of their jobs. They feel very constrained by an over-packed curriculum and inflexible teaching plans, administration and summative assessment demands, and too few opportunities to bring their own ideas forward in order to make the curriculum connect more to their pupils' lives. Because of this factor, they are having to deal day-to-day with pupils who are bored by school work, and the off-task, 'low level' behaviours which result from this. The time has surely come for a rethink of our priorities in Scottish education.

KEY MESSAGES

1 Dewey's and Vygotsky's ideas have especially influenced the development of theories on constructivist and social constructivist learning.

2 Brooks and Brooks (2001) provide a set of constructivist teaching behaviours as a framework within which teachers can experiment. They recognise that there is no one way in which to teach along constructivist lines.

3 Nisbet and Shucksmith (1986) argue that learning to learn must be done in a real context. Therefore the pacing of lessons should accommodate the development of metacognitive skills.

4 According to Resnick (1987), thinking dispositions are cultivated by participation in social communities that value thinking and independent judgement.

5 Emotions and feelings play a crucial role in learning. Boekaerts (1988) distinguishes between 'awareness', and 'willingness' to use personal resources in the service of a learning task.

6 A useful teaching strategy to influence pupils towards holding an incremental view of intelligence (Dweck and Elliott 1983) is to treat errors as natural and useful events rather than as evidence of failure.

7 Biggs (1988) distinguishes between surface, deep and achieving approaches to learning and makes recommendations on how to foster a deep, achieving approach.

8 According to McLean (2003), the teacher's task is to provide the opportunities for achievement that will be motivating. Pupils who are disengaged from learning need alternative learning contexts that start from, and build on, their interests and goals. Learning needs to be connected to their lives, involving real-life challenges and experiences, and be purposeful.

Recommended further reading

Brooks, J.G. and Brooks, M.G. (2001) Becoming a Constructivist Teacher, in Costa, A.L. (ed.) *Developing Minds: A Resource Book for Teaching Thinking* (3rd edition). Alexandria V.A.: Association for Supervision and Curriculum Development.

The authors' descriptors of instructional practices may be of interest.

McLean, A. (2003) *The Motivated School* London: Paul Chapman.

With its emphasis on 'motivation from the inside', this book has important messages for schools. A successful thinking skills intervention should, of course, contribute substantially towards motivating learners 'from the inside'.

Nisbet, J., Shucksmith, J. (1984) *The Seventh Sense* Edinburgh: The Scottish Council for Research in Education

Nisbet, J., Shucksmith, J. (1986) *Learning Strategies* Edinburgh: Routledge Education Books: London

The central role of metacognition in 'learning to learn' is the key theme of both texts. The first is briefer whereas the second provides a more elaborated account.

Perkins, D. (1999) 'The Many Faces of Constructivism', *Educational Leadership*, 57 (3), p.6–11.

The style is accessible and the analysis and arguments unfold in a natural way, leaving you with a lot to think about!

Philips, D.C. and Soltis, J.F. (2004) *Perspectives on Learning*. New York: Teachers College Press.

The introduction states: 'This is a book about theories of learning. In it we want to get you to think about learning–how it happens, and what it is.' Learning and thinking are inextricably linked, therefore it makes sense to be aware of key learning theories and to consider their implications for developing pupils' thinking.

8 Bringing it all together – implementation issues

In this final chapter, there is a more practical focus on how thinking skills approaches can become successfully embedded into school practice. It is structured around three key questions: What are effective approaches to assessing growth in thinking abilities?; What are effective approaches to evaluating thinking skills interventions?; and, What are effective approaches to teachers' continuing professional development (CPD) on teaching thinking? In response to the first question, the discussion draws on current research on formative assessment and focuses on assessment techniques which can be integrated naturally into everyday classroom practice. In response to the second question, some general pointers are provided on methods of designing evaluations for small-scale thinking skills interventions. Finally, a vision in which *creative* and *evidence-informed practice* forms the main cornerstone of teachers' CPD is advanced.

What are effective ways to assess growth in thinking abilities?

Teaching thinking has been taken to mean, in this book, 'guiding and supporting pupils to improve the quality of their thinking, thus enabling them to perform thinking tasks more skilfully.' Therefore by 'growth in thinking abilities' is implied whatever qualitative improvements may be discerned, for example, thinking more *insightfully* or *creatively* about the subject matter in hand.

The lessons from research on formative assessment

There are general principles which apply to assessing any aspect of pupils' learning at school. Marzano (2003) cites a substantial body of research evidence which indicates that academic achievement is considerably higher in classes where effective *formative feedback* is provided to pupils than in classes where it is not. To be effective the feedback must be systematic, timely, and specific to the content being learned since otherwise the results may underestimate the true learning of the pupils.

Inside the Black Box (Black and Wiliam 1998) is a succinct and very readable report on a systematic review of research on assessment for learning. Its starting point is that teaching and learning have to be interactive since teachers need to know about their pupils' progress and difficulties with learning to be able to address their needs. Teachers can find out these needs in a variety of ways – from observation and discussion in the classroom, and from pupils' written work whether done as homework or in class. Black and Wiliam make five key recommendations:

> Feedback to any pupil should be about the particular qualities of his or her work, with advice on what he or she can do to improve, and should avoid comparisons with other pupils.
>
> For formative assessment to be productive, pupils should be trained in self-assessment so that they can understand the main purposes of their learning and thereby grasp what they need to do to achieve.
>
> Opportunities for pupils to express their understanding should be designed into any piece of teaching, for this will initiate the interaction whereby formative assessment aids learning.
>
> The dialogue between pupils and a teacher should be thoughtful, reflective, focused to evoke and explore understanding, and conducted so that all pupils have an opportunity to think and express their ideas.
>
> Tests and homework exercises can be an invaluable guide to learning, but the exercises must be clear and relevant to learning aims. The feedback on them should give each pupil guidance on how to improve, and each must be given opportunity and help to work at the improvement.
>
> (Black and Wiliam 1998: p.9–13)

They point to some detrimental effects on learning when the classroom culture focuses on rewards, such as 'gold stars' or grades. Pupils look for ways to obtain the best marks rather than at their learning needs, and where they have any choice they avoid difficult tasks. They also spend time and energy looking for clues to the 'right answer', and many are reluctant to ask questions out of fear of failure. There is also a negative impact on some pupils' self-esteem and on overall achievement:

Pupils who encounter difficulties and poor results are led to believe that they lack ability, and this belief leads them to attribute their difficulties to a defect in themselves about which they cannot do a great deal. So they 'retire hurt', avoid investing effort in learning which could only lead to disappointment, and try to build up their self-esteem in other ways. Whilst the high achievers can do well in such a culture, the overall result is to enhance the frequency and the extent of under-achievement.

(1998: p.9)

Fortunately such outcomes are not inevitable. The researchers say:

What is needed is a culture of success, backed by a belief that all can achieve. ... Whilst it [formative assessment] can help all pupils, it gives particularly good results with low achievers where it concentrates on specific problems with their work, and gives them both a clear understanding of what is wrong and achievable targets for putting it right. Pupils can accept and work with such messages, provided that they are not clouded by overtones about ability, competition and comparison with others.

(1998: p.9)

Self-assessment is identified as an essential component of formative assessment:

The main problem is ... that pupils can only assess themselves when they have a sufficiently clear picture of the targets that their learning is meant to attain. Surprisingly, and sadly, many pupils do not have such a picture, and appear to have become accustomed to receiving classroom teaching as an arbitrary sequence of exercises with no overarching rationale. It requires hard and sustained work to overcome this pattern of passive reception. When pupils do acquire such overview, they then become more committed and more effective as learners: their own assessments become an object of discussion with their teachers and with one another, and this promotes even further that reflection on one's own ideas that is essential to good learning.

(1998: p.9–10)

Another aspect which is emphasised in the report is the importance of *dialogue* as an opportunity for the teacher to respond to and re-orient the pupil's thinking. Black and Wiliam note occasions where teachers have quite unconsciously responded in ways that would inhibit learning. When the teacher is looking for a particular response, lacks the flexibility or confidence to deal with the unexpected, and then tries to direct the pupil towards giving the expected response, then, over time, '... the pupils get the message – they are not required to think out their own answers' (1998: p.11).

During teacher questioning, when pupils are not given enough quiet time to think out and offer an answer, the quality of responses is poorer overall and those pupils who cannot respond as quickly as others, and who are unwilling to risk making mistakes in public, are excluded from the lesson: 'So the teacher, by lowering the level of questions and by accepting answers from a few, can keep the lesson going but is actually out of touch with the understanding of most of the class – the question-answer dialogue becomes a ritual, one in which all connive and thoughtful involvement suffers.' (1998: p.12).

Thus there are very clear resonances with the themes discussed in the previous chapter, and from this it can be concluded that, if the recommendations of the assessment review are properly implemented, this can contribute substantially towards the development of pupils' thinking.

Approaches to assessment

Swartz and Parks (1994) recommend to teachers that they should use the fourth component of an infusion lesson, *applying thinking*, to assess growth in thinking abilities.

They also suggest asking pupils to use a graphic organiser to record their ideas, making sure they are raising the questions on the thinking map as they try to reach decisions, and if you are having trouble ascertaining this, questioning pupils after they have completed the task.

Thus assessment is conducted in a natural way, as part of the normal course of classroom activities. If approached in this way, it should not create an additional burden for the teacher or pupils, and nor should it have such prominence that pupils are made anxious at the prospect of it. It uses a variety of approaches – written work, teacher observation, teacher questioning, and whatever else is appropriate to the situation. And, of course, the particular thinking skill or process which is being assessed at any particular time has been clearly identified beforehand. A particular strength of the Swartz and Parks approach is that it can be used to assess the integrated use of thinking skills (through problem-solving and decision-making), retention and transfer.

This approach lends itself well to pupils building a *portfolio* in which evidence is accumulated of the growth in their thinking abilities over time. This is a very reliable form of assessment because it does not depend on a 'one off' performance. Also, because the evidence is cumulative, both the teacher and pupil can identify when particular milestones in thinking were achieved. Building a portfolio can be combined with self-assessment, in which pupils select the evidence to go into their portfolios as each item is completed, and give their reasons for including it. A *diary*, completed by the pupil, can accompany the portfolio or be free-standing. A diary can also be a useful tool for teachers to record growth in pupils' thinking abilities (the entries can relate to the class as a whole, a group of pupils or individuals). See Appendix 1 for an example of a pupil and teacher diary.

An approach which already has self-assessment built into is the FourThought Strategy (Tishman, Perkins and Jay 1995) – see Chapter 6, p.103.

Step 1: Before thinking – get ready
Step 2: During thinking – set goals and standards
Step 3: During thinking – keep track of thinking
Step 4: After thinking – reflect

Step 2 is particularly crucial because it enables pupils to consider in advance how they could assess their own or their group's performance on a task objectively, both during and after thinking. This has the effect of making the criteria for a successful performance both shared and public, rather than being in the possession only of the teacher. It also enables pupils to internalise the criteria for high-quality work and to feel more confident about what they are supposed to do.

One way in which the outcomes of step 2 can be set out is in the form of an *assessment rubric*. For example, if the focus of the activity is on accurate prediction, then the following rubric might be produced following discussion in class:

Table 8.01 Sample assessment rubric

Criteria	Accurate prediction Performed well	Scope for improvement
Identifies situation	Considers carefully what he or she already knows about the situation.	Only some important aspects have been considered.
Predicts	Makes a careful prediction in the light of the above.	The prediction involves mostly guesswork rather than weighing up the situation carefully.
Gives reason for prediction	Gives clear, logical reasons for the prediction.	The reasons offered don't seem to relate clearly to the actual situation.
Checks for accuracy	If the actual outcomes of the situation become known, checks to see if the prediction was accurate. In the light of this, evaluates his or her thinking.	Has omitted to do this or reaches the wrong conclusion about the accuracy of the prediction.

A rubric is an especially useful tool for assessing a practical performance, such as a talk or presentation. Furthermore, it can be used to support peer-assessment, tutor-assessment and self-assessment.

Formal tests, such as end-of-topic tests, are part of most teachers' arsenal of assessment techniques once pupils have progressed to the 5–14 levels. Are these suitable for assessing growth in pupils' thinking abilities? The answer to this question is, it depends on the type of questions in the test. If the test focuses more on basic knowledge and skills than on application and problem-solving, then it can provide at best only an indirect measure of growth in pupils' thinking abilities, to the extent that pupils have retained information or learned to perform a skill well as a consequence of having, earlier, engaged in thinking tasks.

A more direct measure can be achieved by designing test questions which require the demonstration of particular thinking skills or processes applied to relevant aspects of the curriculum. Another reason for designing tests in this way is that what is included in the test sends out a clear signal to your pupils about what you, as the teacher, consider to be important. If lessons frequently place a spotlight on the development of thinking, but tests or homework exercises do not reflect this much, pupils will soon get the message that you are not really that serious about supporting the development of their thinking, and they will place their efforts elsewhere. Nisbet (1990) has argued that tests which emphasise the reproduction of factual information can suppress efforts to teach problem-solving and critical reasoning, since tests may have a strong influence on what is taught, how it is taught, and how pupils set about their learning.

It is necessary to ask the right kind of question in the test, one that engages pupils in the kind of thinking that you are seeking directly to assess. Thus, for example, if you are interested in assessing critical thinking skills, then a question in which pupils can *recall arguments which were not the product of the pupils' own thinking* in order to respond to the question is not an adequate measure of critical thinking. The format of the question also makes a difference. While short answer or multiple-choice questions permit specific components of reasoning or thinking to be assessed, they cannot assess the kinds of integrated thinking that are involved in problem-solving or decision-making and nor do they permit pupils to give more elaborated responses in which they can set out their reasoning.

A useful starting point may be to revise test materials to include more open-ended questions which require pupils to, for example, compare and contrast, predict, or generate creative ideas or solutions. This leads to the question of teacher judgement when assessing open-ended tasks. According to Alec Fisher (2001) the teachers' own expertise is key; the teacher must know reasonably clearly what is being looked for in terms of the thinking skill involved, and how it would be demonstrated in a particular discipline or subject area at a particular grade level. If teachers are going to assess pupil thinking in their own discipline, their expertise both in the discipline and in what would count as 'good thinking' is the guarantee of their good judgement. When grading, teachers would take account of the age of the pupils and how much practice they have had at similar tasks. He suggests that teachers can increase their confidence in their judgements by developing model answers or preparing schemes that show what is expected and discussing these with a colleague who knows what the pupils have been taught both in terms of subject matter content and thinking skills.

Beyer (2001) claims that a focused and in-depth approach to assessing a particular thinking skill or process can lead to more accurate information. He proposes a format which consists of six tasks all dealing with the same thinking skill. The first two tasks assess basic knowledge of the skill – its meaning ('Which of the following sentences best defines classifying?') and how you can recognise when someone is doing it ('Which one of these shows information that has been or is being classified?'). The next three tasks assess pupil expertise in executing or performing the skill. The final task assesses pupils' metacognitive understanding of how they execute the skill ('Show me how to classify these objects and explain it to me as you go along'). Beyer claims that the assessment provides specific direct evidence of what the pupil knows and can do to execute the skill, and allows the teacher to judge the degree of proficiency exhibited by the performance and to identify any dysfunctional, irrelevant or erroneous moves, enabling remediation to take place. You may wish to experiment with this approach.

Whatever form the assessment takes, you should try to ensure that when pupils next encounter this particular form of assessment, they will be knowledgeable about how to prepare for it and carry it out well. Thus, if the assessment approach involves pupils in building a portfolio of evidence or folder of work, pupils should be invited to consider in advance questions like:

- Which thinking skills or processes are being focused on?
- What sort of evidence should go in?
- How should the evidence be organised and presented?
- How much evidence is sufficient to demonstrate growth in each thinking skill or process?
- Which criteria and standards will be applied to the work?

Thinking point 1
Consider your current assessment approaches and how well suited they are to assessing growth in pupils' thinking abilities. Modify some of the assessment techniques that you use and/or test out some new approaches.

What are effective ways to evaluate thinking skills interventions?

General pointers

In addition to adopting sound techniques to assess growth in thinking abilities, the following general pointers may be useful for designing and evaluating small-scale thinking skills interventions in your school. This is not a comprehensive list. There are many suitable texts and guides which introduce the key methodologies – action research, case study, evaluation design, and so on.

A requirement is to follow ethical procedures to safeguard the interests of all participants. The British Educational Research Association (BERA) publishes ethical guidelines for educational researchers – see www.bera.ac.uk/publications/guides.php. The Scottish Educational Research Association (SERA) will shortly publish its own guidelines (the present guidelines are being updated) – see www.sera.ac.uk.

1st pointer: Be strategic and systematic in your approach

Don't just dive in with a teaching intervention before having first developed a sound evaluation strategy. Turning your thoughts to evaluation when an intervention is almost over is too late! Perhaps apply the *FourThought* Strategy (Tishman, Perkins and Jay, 1995 – see Chapter 6 p.103).

2nd pointer: Be very clear about your goals

Which questions interest you most about the intervention? Do they concern, for example:

- Its overall effectiveness as a means of developing certain aspects of pupils' thinking (also, which aspects, specifically)?
- The effectiveness of certain features of the intervention (e.g. the use of graphic organisers)?
- Its effectiveness for particular categories of pupils (e.g. low-achieving or high-achieving)?
- Whether pupils are able to transfer the thinking skills to new situations, within or beyond the subject area?
- Whether it fits readily into the existing curriculum?
- Whether it is practical and affordable?
- Its wider impact on your own practice?
- Its wider impact on school policy and practice?

Do not have too many goals in mind otherwise the evaluation will lack any clear focus.

3rd pointer: Decide on what will be taken as firm evidence of success

In relation to each evaluation goal, decide on what will be taken as firm evidence of success. This relates to step 2 of the *FourThought* strategy (see above). A range of measures will be required. In particular, bear in mind the necessity to assess directly the aspects of thinking that the intervention is designed to target.

4th pointer: Enlist the support of interested colleagues

It can be difficult to teach a lesson and observe simultaneously all the interesting events (from the perspective of your evaluation questions) that take place during it. Interested colleagues may be willing to observe and critique some lessons, team teach with you, or become full partners in the evaluation. Furthermore, by involving colleagues in your research, you are beginning to address the problem of 'scaling up' the intervention in future, should it prove to be successful.

5th pointer: Draw on a range of perspectives

Enlist your pupils as full partners in the evaluation by explaining what the intervention is intended to achieve, how it will work, and what their roles will be in the evaluation process. Their opinions of the new method should be systematically taken on board.

Consider whether it would also be useful to get the perspectives of colleagues, parents and school managers.

Consider whether curriculum documents, policy statements and other sources of wider reading (e.g. reports on similar interventions) can cast any further light on issues.

Do not, however, exclude your own perspective. You have particular insights into your pupils' learning needs and an in-depth knowledge of the teaching situation. Since every observer brings their own biases and assumptions to any situation, this is not a good reason for cutting yourself out of the picture.

Do not allow your own opinions to dominate when weighing up the evidence, state your assumptions openly, and do not set out to prove one thing or another (in other words, keep an open mind).

6th pointer: Use efficient methods for data gathering

If the development of thinking features prominently in the curriculum, much of the data that you will need as evidence of growth in pupils' thinking abilities should emerge naturally (from homework exercises, written work done in class, projects, pupils' reviews of their learning, tests and so on), but you *do* need to plan ahead in order to capture it in a useable form, that is, one that can be readily analysed. For example, pupils might write down the main points in their own words following a group or class discussion. Also, most importantly of all, you must 'tame' the exercise – you cannot analyse all of the evidence that your pupils produce!

7th pointer: Evaluate in an ongoing manner and over time

You may decide to gather some 'baseline' measures of pupils' thinking abilities before commencing the intervention, so that you can make a comparison with the stage that pupils have reached by the end.

Allow sufficient time for the new approach to 'bed in' before attempting to reach any firm judgements about its effectiveness.

Do not restrict assessments to summative measures such as end-of-topic tests. Instead gather evidence from formative assessments in an ongoing manner. This can cast light on how *particular facets of the learning and teaching approach* impact on the development of pupils' thinking.

Bear in mind also the need to assess *retention* and *transfer*, which implies evaluating over a longer timescale and perhaps beyond the immediate boundaries of the intervention.

8th pointer: Use valid comparisons

It is natural to want to compare how the 'new' approach compared with the 'old'. To make the comparison as valid as possible, try to compare like with like, in so far as this is achievable. Here is an example:

> Mr McLean has a mixed-ability S3 Standard Grade English class. Pupils are studying imaginative writing. They have to write a short story for their folios. The thinking skills which are being infused into the topic are skills at generating ideas (creative thinking – see Swartz and Parks, 1994). Mr McLean has just finished grading pupils' stories and he has examined the stories also from the perspective of how successful pupils were at generating varied, original and interesting ideas.

Should Mr McLean:

š compare how this class performed in short story writing with how his last year's Standard Grade class performed?

š compare how his class performed in short story writing with how Ms Smith's mixed-ability Standard Grade class performed this year, or with the performance of the year group?

š compare how his class performed in short story writing with how the same class performed a month ago in another form of imaginative writing, writing a letter (taught by him using traditional approaches)?

š compare how one half of his class performed in short story writing (taught using an infusion approach) with how the other half performed (taught using traditional approaches)?

š compare how his class performed in short story writing at the beginning of the intervention (only a brief introduction to short story writing was given by him) with how they performed at the end of the intervention?

and so on.

Try to generate other possibilities which will lead to more valid comparisons.

9th pointer: Think beyond the immediate boundaries of the intervention

Bear in mind one of the messages from earlier chapters about the need to adopt a wider and longer-term perspective. For example, if your intervention is with P2 pupils, how is it to be built upon when your P2 pupils move on to P3 and P4? Or if your intervention is with an S3 English language class on the topic of writing to convey meaning, how is this to be developed across other areas of their curriculum? This is another good reason for involving school colleagues.

10th pointer: Share what you learn from the evaluation

Discuss the findings of the evaluation with your pupils. Also share your findings with colleagues in your school and/or publish a report of your findings (in the *TESS* or a suitable journal, for example). The general idea is to contribute to the body of knowledge that exists about the effectiveness of thinking skills interventions, so that everyone who is interested might benefit from your work! However bear in mind the necessity to be *rigorous* at all stages of conducting the intervention, from planning and preparation through to formulating your conclusions and recommendations.

Thinking point 2
Consider the set of general pointers to designing an evaluation of a thinking skills intervention at the school or classroom level. In particular, think about the issue of making valid comparisons, as exemplified by the scenario about Mr McLean's English class. What other comparisons might he make? Consider what your approach would be.

What are effective approaches to teachers' CPD?

Making good thinking an educational goal has important implications:

> Making good thinking an educational goal affirms that growth in thinking is obtainable by all students. This goal also reflects confidence that all teachers can help students to become better thinkers whatever the learning level, socio-economic background, and culture of the students may be.
>
> (Swartz and Parks 1994: p.3)

The question of how all teachers can help all students to become better thinkers is crucial to address if we are to experience any real success in this big enterprise. It relates to the issue raised in the previous section of how successful thinking skills interventions can be 'scaled up'. All teachers should be sufficiently well informed about the issues to be able to weigh up the various claims put about by the proponents of thinking skills programmes, such as are covered in the recent SCRE review.

Sally Brown, in an address to the General Teaching Council for Scotland (GTCS) argued that the complexities and uncertainties of teaching mean that teachers must constantly monitor and rethink their strategies and be prepared to argue for ideas and principles. Brown claims: 'Teaching is not a matter of getting the 'right' rules but rather a practical matter of learning how to cope with the world of the classroom as it is and of seeing how well our ideas suit our purposes.' (Brown 2001: p.11). From this it can be surmised that any approach which sets out merely to provide rules and procedures for teachers to follow in order to develop pupils' thinking is unlikely to be effective, since the crucial aspects of engagement with ideas and principles and being clear about purposes are underplayed. For the same reason, the typical pack of commercial 'teacher-proofed' classroom resources which sets out thinking activities for pupils to do will generally miss the mark, especially if the teacher has played little part in the selection of the resources for use with his or her class(es).

Lawrence Stenhouse (1980) argued powerfully that the improvement of teaching is not the linear process of the pursuit of obvious goals, rather it is about the growth of understanding and skill of teachers which constitute their resource in meeting new situations and which make old aspirations inappropriate or unattainable. Educational research, on Stenhouse's account, is a process which involves the joint development of educational practice and theory in interaction with each other (Elliott 2001).

Teachers must therefore be in a position to innovate – to test out and refine the theories on teaching thinking and the practical classroom strategies to achieve this. Ultimately they should be able to create sound theories and strategies of their own. In this way, *creative practice* and *evidence-informed practice* become inextricably linked. This fits with Walter Humes' (2001: p.12) proposition that teachers' CPD in Scotland should focus on promoting a better understanding and use of the relationship between abstract theoretical knowledge and situated, experiential knowledge, and that it should, furthermore, encourage teachers to, 'try new ways of working, moving beyond the safe and familiar, even risk-taking.' This is a rather different vision from that put about by some proponents of 'evidence-based teaching', in which teachers, once informed of research evidence on 'what works' in classrooms, are expected to adopt without question a new set of prescriptions.

A more fundamental argument can be posited for the need for all teachers to become immersed in this sort of inquiry; it would be inconceivable (surely!) to seek to put in place a 'thinking curriculum' in schools whilst simultaneously neglecting to create opportunities for teachers to think deeply about how best to nurture their pupils' thinking and learning skills. Put simply, you cannot have a 'thinking curriculum' without thinking teachers. This may seem like a rather obvious point to make, however it would appear that it is not always properly taken on board in the way that teachers are treated. For example, Magdalene Lampert (in Brandt 1994) has criticised how teachers have been treated in North America:

> They've not been treated as people who can and should think
> about curriculum and instruction. They've been treated as people
> who have to be told what to do, who can't think for themselves.
> And that seems particularly ironic when we hear so much about
> trying to get children to think for themselves. (Brandt 1994: p.30)

According to this view, it would appear that teachers' opinions
were not considered as being of much importance for informing
the development of the curriculum and instruction. Schoenfeld
echoes this view in relation to present-day circumstances in US
schools:

> Increasingly, under the assumption that teachers are not well
> enough prepared to be given discretion in the classroom, school
> districts are adopting highly scripted curricula and teachers are
> being held accountable for following the scripts.
>
> (Schoenfeld 2004: p.253)

Is the current situation as experienced by Scottish teachers any
different? According to one teacher, it would appear not. She
returned recently to supply teaching after a career break:

> I had been away from teaching for ten years and when I came
> back that's when I really noticed the change... your first day, your
> first minute in the class you had to do [the prescribed
> mathematics textbook] page such and such with these three
> groups all doing different work ... you didn't have time to sit and
> get to know the children. And I think it was like that in every
> school I went into, everybody was just doing exactly what they
> had been told.

Of course, teachers' experiences will vary considerably depending
on their teaching circumstances and other factors. Hargreaves
contests the idea that teachers should merely 'deliver' the
curriculum, 'They develop it, refine it and interpret it too.' (1992:
p.ix). Even if this latter view is generally held – by teachers
themselves, school managers, designers of the curriculum and
other such like people – there is still the practical issue to be
addressed of time and opportunity for teachers to get together to
work on reshaping the curriculum.

The main focuses of CPD on teaching thinking

In the light of this discussion, what ought the main focuses of CPD on teaching thinking to be?

It should encourage reflection on the appropriateness of the curriculum as a vehicle for enhancing thinking; and encourage teachers to adapt the curriculum in appropriate directions for their pupils.

Also teachers need to be generally knowledgeable about: theories on learning and assessment; ideas on, and strategies for, developing pupils' thinking, including any recent analyses of research findings; and how to design, conduct and evaluate systematic classroom-based inquiries.

Furthermore, teachers need specific knowledge and skills in relation to particular programmes or interventions which are being considered for use with pupils: their purposes, underlying principles, and implementation, including any related research evidence.

Teachers need opportunities, just as their pupils do, to construct their knowledge and understanding actively, sometimes on their own through personal study, but more often within collaborative settings. These settings can be formal, for example, an inservice course or school committee, or informal, for example, a group of close colleagues jointly exploring a thinking skills approach, or a combination of the two. From my analysis, however, it should be evident that a *sustained approach* is necessary for building teachers' understanding, competence and confidence in this field.

The numerous suggestions in this book of practical activities to try out and approaches or ideas to research further should provide ample stimuli for joint exploration with pupils and school colleagues. However, for teachers to feel secure about taking steps towards trying new ways of working and sharing problems of practice or areas of uncertainty, the social setting in schools must be supportive, and teachers questioning pedagogical approaches and school practices and reaching independent judgements must be valued activities (Resnick 1987). Some of the benefits of using a collaborative approach to systematically address problems of practice are discussed by Campbell, Freedman, Boulter and Kirkwood:

> Through engaging in discussion and joint exploration, a range of perspectives can be brought to bear on a problem, leading perhaps to an enriched understanding of the issues. Also, there will be a range of expertise that can be called into play in pursuit of a solution, bringing the possibility for the members of the

group to learn new skills. The potential for cross-fertilisation of ideas and shared planning and development may lead to greater creativity and productivity. The raising of problems informally in discussions with colleagues, or more formally at meetings or in evaluation reports, is an important aspect of working collaboratively, because solutions are often complex and require careful discrimination and judgement. In addition to any direct benefits for the teachers themselves, thinking independently, reflecting critically and openly, problem-solving and collaborating effectively can also model appropriate behaviours and attitudes for their pupils.

(Campbell *et al.* 2003: p.7)

Teachers who are convinced of the need to emphasize thinking skills more may, however, face some difficult challenges:

They have to be determined enough to overcome any resistance from their pupils. They need to establish a classroom discourse which encourages pupils to initiate, speculate and accept that there is not one right answer. They need to maintain this style when there may be pressures to be more didactic and they need to be able to defend and justify their approach in the face of scepticism, indifference and ignorance. It is tempting to speculate that student and newly qualified teachers find the adoption of a new pedagogy easier, because they are not having to abandon conceptualisations and habits that are well entrenched. While this may be so, they probably face a stiffer challenge in relation to socialising forces to which they may be more susceptible.

(Leat 1999: p.398)

Leat illustrates this by referring to one teacher's comments:

I think that it is fair to say that the school is very interested in maintaining its extremely impressive examination record. The ethos of the school is naturally dominated by academic achievement, and one could argue that the pupils are especially anxious in producing correct answers and interpretations ...

(1999: pp.391–2)

Of course, not every teacher is convinced of the need to shift his or her teaching practice in order to place more emphasis on the development of pupils' thinking through using more constructivist teaching approaches, and some teachers are afraid to do so:

their students take comprehensive notes and pass important tests, perform well on worksheets, complete assignments neatly and on time, write well-structured and well-researched individual or group reports, and receive good grades for their work. ...

Becoming a teacher who helps students search rather than follow is challenging and, in many ways, frightening. Teachers who resist constructivist pedagogies do so for understandable reasons: most were not themselves educated in these settings nor trained to teach in these ways.

(Brooks and Brooks 2001: p.151)

Leat (1999) advocates some radically different approaches to inservice education, involving consortia or networks of teachers and schools, in order to counter those factors which tend to undermine innovations in practice. However, I would argue, even with conventional approaches to inservice education, such as a post-graduate course or module, it is possible to build in elements which provide strong support for individual teachers. An online forum can be very effective, for example.

DISCUSSION THREAD ON CHILDREN'S MISCONCEPTIONS

Elizabeth:
With my science class this year I have been really surprised – even shocked – about their misconceptions. During a topic on light, I discovered that a lot of children believe we see because rays from our eyes light up the objects. It follows if children are to begin to understand then it is imperative we correct our pupils' misconceptions first and foremost.

Monica:
I would wholeheartedly agree with you, but how do we help children 'unlearn' these misconceptions? For many of them it is what they have learned from [being] very young children and I find it very difficult to 'convince' them otherwise.

Elizabeth:
Yes, I agree it is a difficult and challenging task to 'undo' children's misconceptions. Teaching mainly science this year, I have learned that no matter what I do, the child will believe or reject a newly introduced idea and that learning takes place as a result of an interaction between my pupils' physical and social environment. This enables them to move on from current ideas to new ones. Through 'hands on' practical investigations, I try to help them check their existing ideas, help them restructure them and then move on in their thinking. Sometimes this doesn't happen in one lesson nor in a series of lessons. I have learned though, to review with the children the extent to which the children's ideas have been developed or changed.

Recently, a group of experienced teachers was able to make considerable progress with embedding thinking skills approaches into their school practice. They were participating in the pilot study of an option module *Learning to Think and Thinking to Learn* as part of the Chartered Teacher Studies course at the University of Strathclyde. It was delivered in partnership with Glasgow City Council and *Tapestry*. Most participants found opportunities to:

- maintain a personal, reflective log in which they reviewed their learning;
- experiment with a range of thinking skills approaches, and develop and evaluate a small-scale classroom-based systematic inquiry;
- work collaboratively with school colleagues through joint development, coaching, team teaching, or asking colleagues to observe lessons and act as a 'critical friend';
- conduct staff development for school colleagues, including support staff;
- produce resources (such as banks of graphic organisers or lesson outlines);
- compile a portfolio of evidence, including commentary on wider reading, which colleagues could read in order to learn more about the approaches; and
- influence departmental or school priorities by having the development of pupils' thinking placed on the development plan.

Key features of the learning environment on the module were (according to participants) that it facilitated interchange of opinions and sharing of experiences, and participants found peers and tutors to be open to ideas, supportive and encouraging of experimentation. Structured learning activities had enabled participants to be more creative when planning lessons and teaching, and to apply ideas from current research to their own teaching practice (Kirkwood and MacKay 2003). Thus participants combined creative practice with evidence-informed practice.

It certainly was not an easy task for participants to achieve all of this! It took considerable effort and a great deal of inventiveness to tailor the approaches to meet the learning needs of their pupils, since the group was drawn from diverse teaching backgrounds, ranging from nursery to secondary stages and mainstream to special education. The personal rewards for participants were however considerable:

> Reminded me that I need to be mentally stimulated and challenged. My students clearly benefited. Enabled me to see another side of my pupils. Reassured me about many aspects of my own practice. Provided an additional means of giving control to my pupils and empowering them. Highlighted areas for research/ improvement/ enrichment. Gave me lots to think about. Highlighted the importance of concrete evidence in assessment. Provided opportunities for making friends with like-minded people.

It is not only experienced teachers who can work very successfully with thinking skills approaches. Secondary student teachers from across subject backgrounds at the University of Strathclyde have found the experience to be very formative in their own learning:

> It is like putting a giant magnifying glass on your teaching methods/ subject content. You see it as it really is – and in most cases you change your approach!

> When planning a lesson – I would ask myself, 'Am I teaching for understanding? Am I encouraging thinking?' While actually teaching I would constantly remind myself of the social/ affective dimension. The placement was lived through this lens.

Being knowledgeable, curious and open to new ideas, caring about the quality of pupils' educational experiences, resilient and inventive are important characteristics for teachers to possess, in order to support the development of their pupils' thinking.

Thinking point 3
Consider your personal CPD needs, in order to support your pupils to become better thinkers.

KEY MESSAGES

1 Effective formative assessment can contribute substantially towards the development of pupils' thinking.

2 Assessment of growth in thinking can be conducted naturally, as part of the normal course of classroom activities, using a variety of approaches, and with a view to assessing retention and transfer. If approached in this way, any additional burden for the teacher or pupils should be minimised.

3 There is a wide range of assessment tools that can be used, including portfolios and diaries (both of which are very valuable for identifying when particular milestones in thinking have been achieved), rubrics (which are especially helpful for assessing practical performances) and formal tests. A cornerstone of effective methods is to develop shared and public criteria for assessment.

4 Formal tests can be designed to gain a direct measure of growth in particular thinking abilities. The question format should permit pupils to give more elaborated responses in which they can set out their reasoning.

5 General pointers for teachers planning to evaluate a school-based thinking skills intervention are: be strategic and systematic; clarify evaluation goals and what will be taken as firm evidence of success; enlist the support of interested colleagues; use a variety of perspectives and efficient methods for data gathering; evaluate in an ongoing manner; use valid comparisons; think beyond the immediate boundaries of the intervention; and share key findings. Any evaluation should be conducted ethically.

6 Being knowledgeable, curious and open to new ideas, caring about the quality of pupils' educational experiences, resilient and inventive are important characteristics for teachers to possess, in order to support the development of their pupils' thinking.

Recommended further reading

Black, P. and Wiliam, D. (1998) *Inside the Black Box: Raising standards through classroom assessment.* London: Kings College London.

This provides an accessible overview of research on assessment for learning.

The *British Educational Research Association* (BERA) publishes three useful guides on educational research **www.bera.ac.uk/publications/guides.php**

Good Practice on Educational Research Writing (2000) – downloadable. Issues and Principles in Educational Research for Teachers (2003) – contact BERA. Revised Ethical Guidelines for Educational Research (2004) – downloadable.

Costa A.L. (2001) ed. *Developing Minds: A Resource Book for Teaching Thinking* (3rd edition). Alexandria V.A.: Association for Supervision and Curriculum Development.

This is a major US edited volume on developing thinking in which a wide range of dimensions is examined. The final section contains seven chapters on various aspects of assessing growth in pupils' thinking. It contains a very useful glossary of thinking terms.

Costa A.L. and Kallick, B. (2004) 'Launching Self-Directed Learners', *Educational Leadership*, 62(1), pp.51–55.

This short article is useful for gleaning ideas on how pupils can be supported and encouraged to assess their own learning and performances over time.

Leat, D. (1999) 'Rolling the Stone Uphill: teacher development and the implementation of Thinking Skills programmes', *Oxford Review of Education*, 25(3), pp.387–403.

This article argues that curriculum development on teaching thinking needs to give much closer attention to teacher development if it is to succeed.

Livingston, K., Soden, R. and Kirkwood, M. (2004) *Post-16 pedagogy and thinking skills: an evaluation*. London: Learning and Skills Research Centre.

As with the Moseley et al. review (see Recommended Reading for Chapter 2), although the title refers to post-16, some aspects of the discussion are also relevant to the school sector, and indeed, recent research on thinking skills interventions conducted in schools is reviewed (see pp.132–135). Section 7 focuses on assessment and evaluation. Section 8 discusses the conditions for successful interventions post-16.

Appendix:

Sample pupil and teacher diary pages

Sample pupil diary page

Diary for [area of curriculum or topic]

Name: Date:

Today/ this week/ in this topic, I really liked ...

_____

These are aspects of my thinking I have improved on.

_____

These are aspects of my thinking I want to improve. I have difficulty with ...

_____

These are some questions I have.

_____

Adapted from Costa and Kallick, 2004

Sample teacher diary page

Teacher: Date:

Child's name, group or class:

I was pleased today/ this week when ...

_____

These are aspects of [child's, group's or class's] thinking in which I have noticed a recent improvement.

_____

These are aspects of [child's, group's or class's] thinking in which I have noticed that some difficulties are being experiencing.

_____

These are some new plans that I have to assist [child, group or class] to overcome these difficulties.

_____

References

Chapter 1

Brandt, R. (2001) 'On Teaching Brains to Think: A Conversation with Robert Sylwester', in Costa, A. L. (ed.) 92001) *Developing Minds: A Resource Book for Teaching Thinking* (3rd edn.), Alexandria V.A.: Association for Supervision and Curriculum Development.

Brooks, J. G. and Brooks, M. G. (2001) 'Becoming a Constructivist Teacher', in Costa, A. L. (ed.) (2001) *Developing Minds: A Resource Book for Teaching Thinking* (3rd edn.), Alexandria V.A.: Association for Supervision and Curriculum Development.

Lipman, M. (2003) *Thinking in Education* (2nd edn.), Cambridge: CUP.

Lowery, L. F. (2001) 'The Biological Basis of Thinking', in Costa, A. L. (ed.) (2001) *Developing Minds: A Resource Book for Teaching Thinking* (3rd edn.), Alexandria V.A.: Association for Supervision and Curriculum Development.

Perkins, D. (2001) 'The Social Side of Thinking', in Costa A. L. (ed.) (2001) *Developing Minds: A Resource Book for Teaching Thinking* (3rd edn.), Alexandria V.A.: Association for Supervision and Curriculum Development.

Perkins, D. (2004) 'Knowledge Alive', *Educational Leadership* 62(1), pp.14–19.

Phillips, D. C. and Soltis, J. F. (2004) *Perspectives in Learning*, New York: Teachers College Press.

Swartz, R. J. and Parks, S. (1994) *Infusing the Teaching of Critical and Creative Thinking into Content Instruction*, Pacific Grove: Critical Thinking Press & Software.

Tishman, S., Perkins, D., and Jay, E. (1995) *The Thinking Classroom: Learning and Teaching in a Culture of Thinking*, Needham Heights, MA: Allyn and Bacon.

Wilson, V. (2000a) *Can thinking skills be taught? A paper for discussion*, Edinburgh: SCRE, www.scre.ac.uk/scot-research/ thinking/.

Chapter 2

Lipman, M. (2003) *See Chapter 1 References*

Marzano, R. J. (2001) 'A New Taxonomy of Educational Objectives', in Costa A. L. (ed.) (2001) *Developing Minds: A Resource Book for Teaching*

Thinking (3rd edn.), Alexandria V.A.: Association for Supervision and Curriculum Development.

Perkins, D. (2001) *See Chapter 1 References*

Presseisen, B. Z. (2001) 'Thinking Skills: Meanings and Models Revisited', in Costa A. L. (ed.) (2001) *Developing Minds: A Resource Book for Teaching Thinking* (3rd edn.), Alexandria V.A.: Association for Supervision and Curriculum Development.

Resnick, L. B. (1987) *Education and Learning to Think* Washington D.C.: National Academic Press.

Resnick, L. B. and Klopfer, L. E. (1989) *Toward the Thinking Curriculum: Current Cognitive Research*, Alexandra V.A.: Association for Supervision and Curriculum Development.

Swartz, R. J. and Parks, S. (1994) *See Chapter 1 References*

Wood, S. (1996) *Victorian Scotland*, Paisley: Hodder Gibson.

Chapter 3

Adey, P. and Sheyer, M. (1994) *Really Raising Standards: Cognitive intervention and academic achievement*, London: Routledge

De Bono, E. (2004) *How to Have a Beautiful Mind*, London: Vermillion.

Fogarty, R. (2001) 'Our Changing Perspective of Intelligence: Master Architects of the Intellect', in Costa A. L. (ed.) (2001) *Developing Minds: A Resource Book for Teaching Thinking* (3rd edn.), Alexandria V.A.: Association for Supervision and Curriculum Development.

Kirkwood, M. J. (2000) 'Infusing higher-order thinking and learning to learn into content instruction: a case study of secondary computing studies in Scotland', *Journal of Curriculum Studies*, 32(4), pp.509–35.

Lipman, M. (1987) 'Some Thoughts on the Foundations of Reflective Education', in Baron, J. B., Sternberg, R. J. (eds.) *Teaching Thinking Skills: Theory and Practice*, New York: W. H. Freeman & Company.

Lipman, M. (2003) *See Chapter 1 References*

Livingston, K., Soden, R. and Kirkwood, M. (2004) *Post-16 Pedagogy and Thinking Skills: an evaluation*, London: Learning and Skills Research Centre.

McGuinness, C. (1999) *From Thinking Skills to Thinking Classrooms: A review and evaluation of approaches for developing pupils' thinking*, Research Brief No. 115, London: HMSO.

Perkins, D. and Salomon, G. (2001) 'Teaching for Transfer' in Costa A. L. (ed.) (2001) *Developing Minds: A Resource Book for Teaching Thinking* (3rd edn.), Alexandria V.A.: Association for Supervision and Curriculum Development.

Perkins, D. (2004) *See Chapter 1 References*

Presseisen, B. Z. (2001) *See Chapter 2 References*

Wilson, V. (2000b) 'Can thinking skills be taught?', *Spotlight No. 79*, Edinburgh: SCRE, www.scre.ac.uk/spotlight/spotlight79

Chapter 4

Holroyd, C. (1989) *Problem Solving and the Secondary Curriculum – A Review for the Scottish Education Department* (unpublished)

McGuinness, C. (2000) 'ACTS: A Methodology for teaching thinking across the curriculum', *Teaching Thinking*, 2, 1–12, www.sustainablethinkingclassrooms.qub.ac.uk/pubs

Nisbet, J. (1990) 'Teaching Thinking: an Introduction to the Research Literature' *Spotlight No. 26*, Edinburgh: SCRE. www.scre.ac.uk/spotlight/spotlight26

Perkins, D. (2004) *See Chapter 1 References*

Perkins, D. and Salomon, G. (2001) *See Chapter 3 References*

Polya, G. (1948) *How to solve it*, Princeton, New Jersey: Princeton University Press.

Resnick, L. B. (1987) *See Chapter 2 References*

Schoenfeld, A. H. (1985) *Mathematical Problem Solving*, London: Academic Press.

Schoenfeld, A. H. (1989) 'Teaching Mathematical Thinking and Problem Solving', in Resnick, L. B. and Klopfer, L. E. (eds.) *Toward the Thinking Curriculum: Current Cognitive Research*, Alexandra V.A.: Association for Supervision and Curriculum Development.

Swartz, R. J. and Parks, S. (1994) *See Chapter 1 References*

Chapter 5

Fisher, R. (1997) *Games for Thinking*, Oxford: Nash Pollock Publishing.

Kirkwood, M. J. (2000) *See Chapter 3 References*

Leat, D. and Higgins, S. (2002) 'The role of powerful pedagogical strategies in curriculum development', *The Curriculum Journal*, 13(1) pp.71–85

Lipman, M. (2003) *See Chapter 1 References.*

Nisbet, J. and Shucksmith, J. (1984) *The Seventh Sense*, Edinburgh: SCRE.

Resnick, L. B. (1987) *See Chapter 2 References*

Schoenfeld, A. H. (1989) *See Chapter 4 References*

Tishman, S., Perkins, D., and Jay E (1995) *See Chapter 1 References*

Chapter 6

McGuinness, C., Sheey, N., Curry, C. and Eakin, A. (2003) *ACTS II Sustainable Thinking Classrooms: A Handbook for Teachers of Key Stage 2 Pupils*, Belfast: Queen's University Belfast

Swartz, R. J. and Parks, S. (1994) *See Chapter 1 References*

Tishman, S., Perkins, D. and Jay, E. (1995) *See Chapter 1 References*

Chapter 7

Biggs, J. (1988) 'The Role of Metacognition in Enhancing Learning', *Australian Journal of Education*, 32(2), pp.127–38.

Boekaerts, M. (1998) 'Emotion, motivation and learning' *International Journal of Educational Research* No. 12 pp. 229–34

Brooks, J. G. and Brooks, M. G. (2001) *See Chapter 1 References*

Dweck, C. S. and Elliott, E. S. (1983) 'Achievement Motivation' in Hetherington, E. M. (ed.) *Socialization, Personality and Social Development*, (Vol. IV of Mussen, P. H. (ed.) *Handbook of Child Psychology*), New York: Wiley.

Entwistle, N. J. (1987) 'Research on Motivation to Learn', *Proceedings of the third meeting of the Forum on Educational Research Motivation in Education: What Role for Research*, Edinburgh: SCRE.

Fisher, R. (1997) *See Chapter 5 References*

Flavell, J. H. (1976) 'Metacognitive Aspects of Problem Solving', in Resnick, L. B. (ed.) (1976) *The Nature of Intelligence*, Hillsdale NJ: Erlbaum.

Fogarty, R. (2001) *See Chapter 3 References*

Goleman, D. (1996) *Emotional Intelligence*, London: Bloomsbury.

Leat, D. and Higgins, S. (2002) *See Chapter 5 References*

McLean, A. (2003) *The Motivated School*, London: Paul Chapman.

Nisbet, J. (1990) *See Chapter 4 References*

Nisbet, J. and Shucksmith, J. (1984) *See Chapter 5 References*

Nisbet, J. and Shucksmith, J. (1986) *Learning Strategies*, Edinburgh: Routledge Education.

Perkins, D. (1999) 'The Many Faces of Constructivism', *Educational Leadership*, 57(3), pp.6–11.

Perkins, D. (2001) *See Chapter 1 References*

Perkins, D., and Salomon, G. (2001) *See Chapter 3 References*

Phillips, D. C. and Soltis, J. F. (2004) *See Chapter 1 References*

Pollard, A. (2002) *Reflective Teaching: Effective and Evidence-informed Professional Practice*, London: Continuum.

Polya, G. (1948) *See Chapter 4 References*

Resnick, L. B. (1987) *See Chapter 2 References*

Schoenfeld, A. H. (1989) *See Chapter 4 References*

Swartz, R. J. and Park, S. (1994) *See Chapter 1 References*

Tishman, S., Perkins, D. and Jay, E. (1995) *See Chapter 1 References*

Vygotsky, L. S. (1978) Mind in Society. *The Development of Higher Psychological Processes* Cambridge MA: Harvard University Press.

Chapter 8

Beyer, B. K. (2001) 'A Format for Assessing Thinking Skills', in Costa, A. L. (ed.) (2001) *Developing Minds: A Resource Book for Teaching Thinking* (3rd edn.), Alexandria V.A.: Association for Supervision and Curriculum Development.

Black, P. and Wiliam, D. (1998) *Inside the Black Box: Raising standards through classroom assessment*, London: Kings College London.

Brandt, R. (1994) 'On Making Sense: A Conversation with Magdalene Lampert', *Educational Leadership*, February 1994, pp.26–30.

Brooks, J. G. and Brooks, M. G. (2001) *See Chapter 1 References*

Brown, S. (2001) 'What is teaching for?', *Teaching Scotland*, Edinburgh: General Teaching Council for Scotland.

Campbell, A., Freedman, E., Boulter, C. and Kirkwood, M. (2003) *Issues and Principles in Educational Research for Teachers*, Notts: British Educational Research Association.

Costa, A. L. and Kallick, B. (2004) 'Launching Self-Directed Learners', *Educational Leadership*, 62(1), pp.51–5.

Elliott, J. (2001) 'Making evidence-based practice educational', *British Educational Research Journal*, 27(5), pp.554–74.

Fisher, A. (2001) 'Assessing Thinking Skills' in Costa, A. L. (ed.) (2001) *Developing Minds: A Resource Book for Teaching Thinking* (3rd edn.), Alexandria V.A.: Association for Supervision and Curriculum Development.

Hargreaves, A. (1992) 'Foreword', in Hargreaves, A. and Fullan, M. (eds.) *Understanding Teacher Development*, London: Cassell.

Humes, W. (2001) 'Conditions for professional development', *Scottish Educational Review*, 33(1), pp.6–17.

Kirkwood, M. and MacKay, E. (2003) *Evaluation of Learning to Think and Thinking to Learn: A Pilot Study of an Option Module for the Scottish Chartered Teacher Programme*, Glasgow: University of Strathclyde.

Leat, D. (1999) 'Rolling the Stone Uphill: teacher development and the implementation of Thinking Skills programmes', *Oxford Review of Education*, 25(3), pp.387–403.

Marzano, R. J. (2003) *What works in Schools: Translating research into action*, Alexandria V.A.: Association for Supervision and Curriculum Development.

Nisbet, J. (1990) *See Chapter 4 References*

Perkins, D. (1999) *See Chapter 7 References*

Resnick, L. B. (1987) *See Chapter 2 References*

Schoenfeld, A. H. (2004) 'Multiple learning communities: students, teachers, instructional designers and researchers', *Journal of Curriculum Studies*, 36(2), pp.,237–255

Stenhouse, L. (1980) 'Reflections', in Stenhouse, L. (ed.) *Curriculum Research and Development*, London: Heinemann.

Swartz, R. J. and Parks, S. (1994) *See Chapter 1 References*

Tishman, S., Perkins, D. and Jay, E. (1995) *See Chapter 1 References*

Index